DICKINSON LECTURERS

1936–1937

GEORGE O. MAY

Partner; Price, Waterhouse & Co., New York

IMPROVEMENTS IN FINANCIAL ACCOUNTS

(*Privately printed*)

1937–1938

Sir LAURENCE HALSEY

Partner; Price, Waterhouse & Co., London

THE POSITION OF THE PUBLIC ACCOUNTANT IN RELATION TO BUSINESS AND GOVERNMENT IN GREAT BRITAIN

(*Privately printed*)

1939–1940

WILLIAM A. PATON

Professor of Accounting, University of Michigan

RECENT AND PROSPECTIVE DEVELOPMENTS IN ACCOUNTING THEORY

(*Business Research Study No. 25, Harvard University Graduate School of Business Administration*)

1940–1941

WALTER A. STAUB

Partner; Lybrand, Ross Bros. & Montgomery, New York

AUDITING DEVELOPMENTS DURING THE PRESENT CENTURY

(*Published by the Harvard University Press*)

AUDITING DEVELOPMENTS DURING THE PRESENT CENTURY

LONDON : HUMPHREY MILFORD
OXFORD UNIVERSITY PRESS

AUDITING DEVELOPMENTS DURING THE PRESENT CENTURY

BY

WALTER A. STAUB

Dickinson Lecturer, 1940–1941

CAMBRIDGE · MASSACHUSETTS
HARVARD UNIVERSITY PRESS
1942

PRINTED AT THE HARVARD UNIVERSITY PRINTING OFFICE
CAMBRIDGE, MASSACHUSETTS, U. S. A.

HARVARD UNIVERSITY
GRADUATE SCHOOL OF BUSINESS ADMINISTRATION
GEORGE F. BAKER FOUNDATION

DICKINSON LECTURES IN ACCOUNTING

IN January 1929 the Arthur Lowes Dickinson Fund was established at the Harvard Graduate School of Business Administration by the firm of Price, Waterhouse & Co. "in recognition of the debt due by the accounting profession in general, and particularly by this firm, to a former partner, Sir Arthur Lowes Dickinson." The income from this Fund was for a number of years used exclusively for the purpose of conducting research in the field of accounting. In 1936 the provisions of the Fund were modified to provide that "in addition there may from time to time be appointed, for one year, a man outstanding in Accounting who shall deliver at the Graduate School of Business Administration one or more lectures, and shall be designated as Dickinson Lecturer."

FOREWORD

THE lectures contained in this work constitute the fourth series of the Dickinson Lectures in Accounting at the Harvard Graduate School of Business Administration. Since the earlier series dealt with the development of Accounting in the United States and Great Britain, and with the present status of its principles, it seems particularly desirable that the present lectures should concern themselves with the analytical and review branch of the general topic, the problems of Auditing, since, especially in recent years, they have undergone radical changes.

The name of Walter A. Staub is well and favorably known wherever accounting and auditing problems are considered. He represents the best type of American professional businessman. Not only is he a master of the techniques of his profession, with a firm grasp on its principles, but he has demonstrated outstanding perspicacity in understanding the significance of the results of accounting analysis, and has revealed a judicial comprehension of the equities involved, areas which constitute the special province of the independent public accountant. The Securities and Exchange Commission has more and more insisted upon the independence of the public accountant in this type of activity because of the importance of the pronouncements.

These lectures are a clarification of the developments in auditing theory and practice in the light of a long lifetime of experience in an environment where they could be most advantageously witnessed.

ARTHUR W. HANSON

Harvard University
August, 1942

CONTENTS

AUDITING DEVELOPMENTS DURING THE PRESENT CENTURY

INTRODUCTION

It was with especial pleasure that I accepted the invitation to serve as the lecturer on the Dickinson Foundation in 1941 because of the very high regard which I have for the memory of the late Sir Arthur Lowes Dickinson, in whose honor the Arthur Lowes Dickinson Foundation in the Graduate School of Business Administration of Harvard University was established.

It was my privilege to become acquainted with him while I was still very young in the public practice of accounting. I last saw him in 1933 at the International Congress on Accounting in London when, in bringing the greetings and good wishes of the New York State Society of Certified Public Accountants to the Congress, I had the opportunity to express the indebtedness of our profession in America for the guidance given it by Sir Arthur in the early nineteen hundreds. He was a worthy exemplar of those ideals and objectives which he so wisely and persuasively urged upon the young profession in that vital and growing period of forty years ago.

My appearance before you today coincides approximately with the completion of forty years of my activity as a public accountant, first as a member of the staff of my firm and for thirty years as a partner with those who founded it. I shall seek to present some of the developments of that period in complying with the request that I devote these lectures to a consideration of some phases of the subject of auditing.

Since a considerable portion of the independent public accountant's audit work consists of so-called balance sheet audits or examinations, I shall discuss with you some of the developments relating to work of the accountant in performing engagements of that character. Also, I shall seek to identify some of the major influences responsible for these developments.

Auditing has been sometimes described as the analytical phase of the accountant's work and accounting *per se* as the synthetic phase. In practice the line between the two often becomes very dim; in fact, that line is frequently not apparent at all because of the overlapping of the two phases. The form of auditor's report or certificate recommended by the American Institute of Accountants for use in normal circumstances refers to the accountant's examination and tests of the records underlying the financial statements, but also it includes an opinion that the statements set forth the position of the company and the results of its operations "in conformity with generally accepted accounting principles applied on a basis consistent with that of the preceding year."

Robert H. Montgomery, in the sixth edition of his work on *Auditing Theory and Practice*, describes a balance sheet audit or examination as comprising "the minimum examination of the financial statements, system of internal control, accounting procedures, accounting records, and other supporting evidence, which the auditor believes is appropriate in the particular case and in accordance with generally accepted auditing procedure to enable him to express an opinion as to the position of the company, the results of its operations for a period, and the conformity of the balance sheet and statements of income and surplus with generally accepted principles of accounting consistently applied."[1]

Further, he lays down the principles or rules of a balance sheet audit or examination, which indicate but do not limit the audit phase of the accountant's work, as follows:

Balance sheet audits are not all alike in the nature and extent of the work because of the variations in the kinds of business encountered and

[1] New York, The Ronald Press Company, 1940, p. 8.

in the systems of internal check and control in use, but the procedures followed by the auditor should be designed to give him reasonable grounds for belief:

1. That, except as otherwise noted, all the assets shown in the balance sheet were actually owned by the client at the balance sheet date and were carried at amounts arrived at by application of generally accepted accounting principles;
2. That there were no other assets of a material amount which were not, but which should have been, shown;
3. That the liabilities shown in the balance sheet were actual or contingent liabilities;
4. That all liabilities of materiality are expressed in the balance sheet;
5. That the nature of surplus is adequately disclosed, that the statement of income is reasonably classified and informative, and that there is no substantial misstatement of the net income for the period;
6. That the capital stock is properly classified and stated, and that no stock of any class has been issued in excess of amounts duly authorized.[1]

One of the best comments I have seen on what might be called the accounting phase of auditing, and which is all the more interesting because of its coming from outside the accounting profession, is the following portion of the report made in 1939 by the New York Stock Exchange's Stock List Subcommittee on Independent Audits and Audit Procedure:

> . . . there seem to be those who, when faced with certain inevitable limitations and qualifications in the audit phase, entertain doubts as to the value of the entire independent audit. They seem for the moment to overlook the importance of the accounting phase. This is partly, of course, the result of the recent McKesson & Robbins case, in which the fraud rested on the falsity of the factual matter which is the basis of all accounts. It may be worth noting, however, that a distortion of emphasis may result also from a circumstance of terminology; the same word "audit" is used for the entire procedure, and also for one of its two phases . . . .
>
> . . . financial statements of industrial companies are not statistical

[1] *Ibid.*, pp. 8–9.

presentations of fact fixed in the form which the stockholder reads. While properly based on facts, these statements represent the judgments of the Company's management in the application of conventional methods of stating assets and liabilities and in appropriate allocations of income and outgo items to specific periods of time. For example, plant and property are usually stated on the basis of cost, or on some other conventional basis — and not at a figure supposed to reflect present day value. Other items are usually stated at going concern values, and profits are calculated on this basis.

The importance of a periodic review by outside experts to see that these numerous judgments have been made in accordance with accepted accounting principles consistently followed by the Company must be apparent to every one — entirely apart from any methods the business world may employ to assure itself of the authenticity of the data underlying the accounts. The independent public accountant is thoroughly qualified to make such a review. For this he has been specially trained. The public is entitled to rely upon his opinion regarding the soundness and consistency of the accounting judgments made by the Company in the preparation of its reports to stockholders. If the independent public accountant does not concur in the results of these judgments, he will take exception to the Company's method by a statement in his auditor's opinion accompanying the financial statements. If his exception is of sufficient importance, he will express no opinion, and explain in his report why it is withheld. The independent public accountant's opinion on the soundness of judgments and consistency of methods is of real importance — for even with correct factual data at the base, the possibilities of accounting errors and misrepresentations are very great.

In an address by John Haskell, Vice President of the New York Stock Exchange, in 1939, on "What Is Expected of the Independent Auditor from the Viewpoint of the Investor," he made the following statement — again interesting because expressed by a layman:

The New York Stock Exchange believes that the investor expects many things of the independent auditor, but first I shall mention some which we believe should not be expected. We do not expect the auditor to make a detailed verification of all transactions of listed companies. We do not expect him to be a superman or detective endowed with the second sight of catching — from his examination of the books and such tests and checks as he may make of the records to the underlying data

— every minor defalcation that may have been committed. We do not expect him to qualify as a general appraiser or valuation expert of all the countless materials which go to make up the stream of commerce and industry.

On the other hand, the Exchange and the investor do expect that the independent auditor will not permit the use of his name in connection with a report on which the public may rely if any restrictions are imposed upon his freedom of access to any of the records or information which he considers necessary in order to express his professional opinion that the financial statements present fairly the position of the Company and the results of its operations.

We expect the independent public accountant to make an audit study to satisfy himself of the adequacy and effectiveness of the Company's system of internal control.

We expect that, by test checks and methods of sampling and observation, the auditor will go beyond the books of record to satisfy himself of their conformity with the underlying facts.

We expect the auditor to apply sound judgment so that, over a period of time, and irrespective of the emphasis of the day on certain items, all phases of the Company's business will be covered. The investor relies upon the impression created by the financial statements as a whole and it is obvious that a well-rounded audit offers greater safeguards than one in which excessive emphasis is placed on certain phases to the neglect of others.

The Exchange and the investor expect the independent public accountant to be independent in fact as well as in name.

We count upon his having wide experience, professional competency and a detached, unbiased viewpoint. We expect and demand of all professional honesty and the highest personal integrity.

Aside from the auditing of the records themselves, the Exchange and the investor expect that the independent auditor will continue to assume great responsibility as to the accounting judgments which govern the final results set forth in financial statements, so that these judgments may be in accordance with generally accepted sound accounting principles.

We expect the independent auditor to be particularly alert to maintain basic distinction between capital and income in the preparation of reports to stockholders. From the viewpoint of the investor, even more than from the viewpoint of short-term creditors and others, the cardinal importance of the earnings statement must be emphasized. Safeguards must be provided against misstatements of earnings by the absorption of losses which should be made against income through charges to capital or capital surplus, earned surplus or by other methods that violate this basic distinction.

Although we do not expect the auditor's report to guarantee financial statements, we expect it to set forth an opinion upon which the auditor is willing to stake his professional reputation that he has satisfied himself that his examination has been as extensive as the general standards of his profession have established and that, beyond this, he has satisfied himself, by methods and to the extent deemed appropriate, that the financial statements fairly present the position of the Company and the results of its operations in accordance with sound accounting principles.

We believe that the investor expects the auditor's certificate or report accompanying the completed financial statements to be as clear, concise, unequivocal and illuminating as your professional ability can make it. It should make clear, in language the investor understands, the distinction between statements and phrases included by way of explanation for the added information of the investor and any exceptions to the data in the financial statements or in the methods used in their preparation with which the accountant is not in full accord.

Finally, we expect the independent auditor and his profession to lead in the development of effective methods and progressive steps in the constant evolution of sound and more understandable reports. Federal statutes and rules and the variegated, conflicting, over-lapping crazy-quilt of local regulations establish minimum standards with which all must comply, but the investor expects that corporations whose securities are listed on the New York Stock Exchange will observe much higher standards. He counts on your profession to see to it that, in the field of audits and reports, added safeguards and constant development of sound practices will surpass the minimum standards which must apply to all.

I. HISTORICAL DEVELOPMENTS

I recall that in the early days of my work in the office of my firm the usual audit which we were called upon to make was focused largely on an examination of the cash records, the comparison of paid checks with the recorded expenditures (either directly with the cash book, if the accounts were so organized that this could be readily done, or first with the check stubs for one or more bank accounts and then the check stubs with the cash book), examination of petty cash vouchers, checking of postings from customers' ledger accounts to the receipt side of the cash book, comparison of deposits per the check book with the cash book, and, naturally, reconciling of bank balances between bank pass book and cash book, a count of the petty cash on hand, and such other examinations as in the circumstances of the particular client seemed to afford a basis for the most thorough verification of the integrity of the cash accounts. Those features of the accounts which, in the modern audit, require so much time and attention, such as the testing and review of receivables, not only to ascertain their existence but, even more, their probable collectibility, the examination of the inventories, and the review of depreciation and depletion allowances, received proportionately a lesser part of the accountant's time than today.

There were various reasons for this: (1) many of the concerns under audit were of moderate size, the ownership was closely held and frequently in the hands of the management, and the primary purpose of the examination was to give a sort of clearance to the treasurer or cashier, or whoever was acting in a position of trust in respect to the funds of the concern, so that the owners might be assured on that point; (2) in comparatively few instances were financial statements certified for the purpose of filing them with banks to obtain credit or for publication to stockholders; (3) the periodic determination of profit or loss on a consistent basis was not yet emphasized as it is today; (4) among a great many businessmen there was, as yet, no recognition of the need for care in following sound accounting principles in the preparation of their financial statements. Those who were conservatively minded naturally had their accounts kept on that basis and in some cases kept their accounts on an ultraconservative basis. Those who were unduly optimistic and of that class who, like Micawber, were always looking forward to something turning up to make it possible for them to dispose of stock which had been on hand a long time without finding a customer, did not like to have their style cramped by being reminded of the need for dealing realistically with the inventory and writing down such items from cost to a figure more nearly approaching realizability. Not infrequently the bankruptcy court took care of their situation before they had become converted to the desirability of following sound principles in the keeping of their accounts.

Changes in Trends of Auditing

With the rapid growth of American business following the Spanish-American War, the increase in the size of many enterprises (sometimes through consolidation with others, as during the trust forming period of the late eighteen nineties and the early twentieth century), and the auditing of larger concerns, there developed the necessity for making the audit one of selected tests of the accounts rather than an endeavor to examine all of the transactions of the period even in the cash account.

The newer approach was primarily that which has come to be known as the balance sheet examination, viz., substantiation, so far as practicable, of all items, both assets and liabilities, entering into the balance sheet, and a general review of the operating accounts for the period intervening since the last previous annual audit, together with a comparison of the various revenue and expense groups with the corresponding operating accounts of the previous period or periods, inquiry into the causes for marked fluctuations, and such tests of the items entering into the operating accounts as seem appropriate in the circumstances of the particular engagement. Especially in those cases where the examination was for the purpose of submitting a certified balance sheet to a bank for credit purposes, the audit of the items entering into the operating accounts as distinguished from balance sheet items was frequently quite limited, though even there the experienced accountant recognized the light that would be thrown on the balance sheet position from a test examination of the operating accounts.

One result of this development was more and more emphasis on the importance of the accountant's review of the manner in which the management had dealt with the recording and classification of transactions of the company from the standpoint of the application of sound accounting principles and the consequent dependability of the determination of income and presentation of financial position.

During the decade preceding the First World War, the banking credit of commercial concerns was increasingly being based not alone on good character but also on a more definite knowledge by the lending bank of the financial affairs of the borrower. In the large cities the commercial banks were establishing credit departments which studied with care the financial statements[1] filed with them by borrowers and supplemented the statements with such information concerning the nature of the borrower's business organization and other features of the concern as they could learn. Credit

[1] The development was, first, the filing of unaudited statements prepared by borrowers and, later, the filing of certified statements in compliance with the requirements of the lending banks and of the Federal Reserve Banks.

men in the banks were perhaps the earliest group outside the accountancy profession which recognized and supported the now generally accepted accounting principle of valuing inventories at cost or market, whichever is lower. They recognized that it is a principle born, not out of pure logic, but rather out of long business experience and observation. They grasped the principle that it is wise to provide for potential losses, and not to count your chickens before they are hatched. The banker's experience has taught him that by some strange perversity of fate potential losses much oftener become actual than is true of possible profits. Hence they became firm believers in writing down inventories when the price level fell below cost but not in writing them up when market prices rose. This principle is so widely recognized today that it is difficult to realize that only a few decades ago many businessmen clung firmly to the idea that if it was sound practice to write down inventories in a falling market, it was just as sound to write them up in a rising market.

The increasing use during the present century of certified financial statements in bankers' prospectuses for security offerings emphasized still more the need for the auditor majoring on such questions as inventory valuations and their reflex action on the determination of annual operating profits, the allowance to be made for possible loss on receivables, the allowances for depreciation of plant and exhaustion of wasting assets, the ascertainment, so far as possible, of all direct and contingent liabilities, the disclosure of write-ups of property and credits to surplus arising therefrom, and so forth.

An influence which contributed much to the improvement of accounting practices and strengthened the hand of the public accountant who had long been urging such improvement arose out of the taxes imposed during the First World War. It was a very practical influence because in so many cases it appealed to the business pocketbook. So long as income taxes were at a low rate they had little effect on the accounting practices of business concerns. When, however, in 1917 income taxes were materially increased and a heavily graduated excess profits tax was enacted and for the following year a still heavier war profits tax was imposed, with a further increase in the rates of income tax, business concerns became receptive to such suggestions as stating inventories on a conservative basis and making adequate allowances for depreciation of the plant.

Prior to this time the depreciation policies of many industrial concerns had been on the hit or miss order, where indeed there was not an utter absence of depreciation allowances. There were still quite a few businessmen who were contending that, as long as they were maintaining their plants in good operating condition, renewals and replacements were a sufficient offset to the depreciation allowance which accountants had been urging upon them. In some cases, where ultra-conservative management had been absorbing in operating expenses costs of expansion of the plant, this might have been the case, but there were many others where the argument was fallacious; the auditor, however, could do little except bring out the facts in his report and qualify it accordingly.

The incidence of high taxes completely changed the picture. Businessmen were now ready to recognize the applicability of the inventory principle of cost or market, whichever is lower, and many a concern about that time established a reasonably consistent depreciation policy which has been followed since. The United States Treasury does not have the same broad powers to prescribe accounting methods as does a regulatory body like the Interstate Commerce Commission. Its indirect influence, however, has been very considerable because the business concern that pursues a less conservative policy in its accounts in respect of matters like inventory and plant depreciation than it claims in its tax returns is at a decided disadvantage from a tax standpoint, and this is generally recognized.

The accounting necessary under government contracts during the First World War, particularly those on the cost-plus basis, gave a stimulus born of necessity to better accounting methods. It paralleled and reinforced the influence of high taxes in leading to adoption of sounder inventory methods, better costing systems, departmentalized accounting, recognition of plant depreciation as an element of manufacturing cost, and the like. It was but natural that this practice led to calling on the public accountant for advice and guidance. In many cases, too, this led to the periodical auditing of the accounts.

One of the most helpful influences in furthering the practice of having published financial statements accompanied by certificates of independent public accountants was that exerted by the New York Stock Exchange. As the culmination of informal activity in this direction for some years, the president of the Exchange on January 6, 1933, made an announcement that since April of 1932 all corporations applying for listing of their securities had been asked to include in their listing agreements an undertaking that future annual financial statements, published more than three months after the agreement, would be audited by independent public accountants and accompanied by a certificate of such accountants, setting forth the scope of the audit and qualifications, if any, made by them in respect thereto, and that the Committee on Stock List had considered many reasons advanced why this procedure should not apply in particular cases but had made exceptions only in the case of certain railroad companies. The announcement further stated that after July 1, 1933, all listing applications, excepting for the time being railroad companies reporting to the Interstate Commerce Commission, would have to contain a certificate of independent accountants as to the balance sheet, income statement, and surplus statement for the most recent fiscal year, and an agreement that annual reports to stockholders would thereafter be audited and accompanied by a similar certificate.

Especially from the time that Mr. J. M. B. Hoxsey became executive assistant to the Stock List Committee of the Exchange during the 1920's, the Exchange had been doing its utmost to encourage the preparation of financial statements published by listed corporations on the basis of sound accounting principles. The support of the Exchange in this way, which antedated the enactment of the securities acts, was most helpful to accountants in their efforts for improvement in corporate accounting practice. The services of Mr. Hoxsey, representing the Exchange, in accounting conferences with the officers of listed corporations, with the independent accountants examining the statements of such corporations, and with the Committee of the American Institute of Accountants on Cooperation with Stock Exchanges, were of the greatest value in furthering the recognition and adoption by corporations of sound accounting principles and the improvement in form and content of published statements.

Influence of Regulatory Bodies

The increasing demand for accountants' services, and the changes in trend of the type of auditing service rendered, which I have just mentioned, lead us to consider the influence on accounting practice which governmental bodies have had in recent decades and which have naturally had a bearing on the work of the independent accountant as an auditor. The Interstate Commerce Act of 1906 gave the Commission authority to prescribe, not only uniform annual reports to the Commission, which it had had the power to do for some twenty years previously, but also the accounts to be kept, any deviation from which was forbidden. This had a decided influence on railroad accounting and has caused a higher degree of standardization of accounting in that field than in any other branch of industry or commerce. Also, the Commission recognized that some of its earlier instructions for the preparation of reports to it had not been based on sound accounting principles; for instance, the Commission had formerly permitted bond discount to be charged to property account but in its new classification of construction expenditures recognized the force of the accountant's contention that discount is nothing else than interest paid in advance and consequently should not be permanently capitalized. On another question, i.e., that of allowances for depreciation of property, the Commission has never gone to the full length to which industrial concerns as a whole have come during the last quarter century. It has made depreciation allowances compulsory for equipment but not for track or structures.

Incidentally, I happened to note in the first edition of Montgomery's *Auditing Theory and Practice* the following extract from an article in a financial paper, which is of interest because of the points mentioned which have significance in the auditing of railroad accounts:

> No one doubts that the Baltimore and Ohio of today is a magnificent property. But that is all the more reason why it should seem very strange that some of those who are still in the board should apparently have forgotten the experience of sixteen years ago. Early in September of 1896, despite the profit and loss surplus of $23,737,000 then existing, Stephen Little was employed to go over the old Baltimore and Ohio's books. Before the end of that month the announcement that a receiver had been appointed for the company came like a bolt out of the blue. In his report Mr. Little gave the following causes for the Baltimore and Ohio's trouble:
>
> 1. The inflation or overstatement of net income,
> 2. The mischarge of worn-out equipment to profit and loss,
> 3. The capitalization of charges to income,
> 4. The capitalization of so-called improvements and betterments of leased lines,
> 5. The payment of unearned dividends,
> 6. The understatement of liabilities, etc.[1]

[1] New York, The Ronald Press Company, 1912, p. 430.

It is of interest to note that not one of the six "causes for the Baltimore & Ohio's trouble," which are stated above and in respect of which the company's books were not, in Mr. Little's opinion, on a sound basis, implied any monetary dishonesty but represented a failure to apply sound accounting principles.

The Interstate Commerce Commission has apparently had little influence on the development of accounting principles or practice outside the railroad field. So far as the public accountant is concerned, the effect of the authoritative powers of the Interstate Commerce Commission in respect of railroad accounting has apparently been to discourage the use of the public accountant's services by the railroads. This has probably been due in part at least to the erroneous impression which has gotten abroad that the Commission periodically audits the accounts of the railroads.

The Securities Act of 1933 specifically exempts from its provisions "any security issued by a common carrier which is subject to the . . . Interstate Commerce Act. . . ." Hence, the financial statements included in prospectuses of railroad security offerings are not required to be certified by independent public accountants.

A drastic criticism of the status of railroad accounting after three decades of governmental regulation was expressed by Jules I. Bogen, editor of the New York *Journal of Commerce*, in a paper read before the American Management Association in 1939. The paper, which was entitled, "An Objective Appraisal of the Independent Audit," contained the following paragraph dealing with one of the numerous hasty suggestions made as the result of the shock of the McKesson & Robbins case:

> Thirdly, it has been proposed that a federal statute be passed setting up auditing and internal management check standards for all corporations engaged in interstate commerce. Now there is one industry where accounting has been subject to such federal regulation since 1906 — the

railroad industry. And if there is any type of accounting which requires really fundamental reform, it is railroad accounting. If that is what rigid government regulation of accounting does, I think it is the last thing we want.

It is of interest to note in passing some marked divergences between the developments in railroad accounting and those occurring in the industrial and mercantile field during the past quarter-century. Illustrative instances are (a) the treatment of surplus charges and credits, and (b) allowances for depreciation of property.

In the financial statements of industrial concerns it has become more and more the practice to absorb in the current income account items which under the practice of an earlier day would have been shown as direct charges or credits to the surplus account because of having had their origin in transactions of a prior period, because of being considered nonrecurring, or for some other reason. Where the items are of large amount, the current net income may be first stated and the special or extraordinary items, if of large amount, deducted from or added thereto. In the published statements of railroads, however, the profit and loss account (equivalent in effect to the account more generally termed surplus in industrial accounting) is still the account to which such items are directly charged or credited, despite the fact that over a period of years they have an important effect on the net income of the period.

In a recent railroad prospectus the net income of a guarantor railroad corporation was shown for each year of the past decade. Following was a statement of the net debits charged directly to Profit and Loss for each year of the decade. The annual net income amounts for the ten years aggregated approximately $53,000,000, and the net debits to Profit and Loss some $20,000,000. A part of the latter amount was of a special character, such as retirement losses arising out of a rearrangement of certain facilities for joint operation thereafter with another railroad, but a substantial portion represented write-offs of advances apparently made to finance current losses of such joint operation and net debits for retired road and equipment.

The net debits for retired road and equipment appear to have arisen out of the absence of any obligatory requirement for setting up allowances for depreciation of roadway and structures, though the Commission has required such allowances to be set up currently for depreciation of rolling stock since the promulgation by it of the classification of accounts which became effective in 1907.

The annual net income shown as such would apparently have been materially less had some of the items charged or credited directly to Profit and Loss been treated in the same manner as has become general practice among industrial companies.

Another illustrative instance which might be mentioned is the 1940 annual report of a railroad company which showed a net profit of approximately $200,000 in its Income Account, net debits of almost $900,000 to Profit and Loss Account for Retired Road items, and miscellaneous credits and debits amounting, net, to a credit of somewhat less than $500,000. There is no explanation in the Profit and Loss Account as to whether the Retired Road amount includes any extraordinary items such as abandonments. This is one of the railroads the financial statements of which are accompanied by a certificate of independent accountants. The certificate stated the opinion that, subject to certain considerations not here material, the ". . . balance sheet and related statements of income and profit and loss fairly present, *in accordance with the requirements of the Interstate Commerce Commission*, the financial condition of the Company . . . and the results of its operations . . ." (italics supplied).

About the time of the enactment of the Interstate Commerce Act of 1906 there was an acceleration of the movement for regulation of public utilities other than the railroads, including street railways, electric light and power companies, and gas companies. This regulation came from the various states, and came earlier in some than in others. Also, the reaction on accounting methods of the utilities varied in different states. The regulatory acts in some states gave power to commissions to prescribe the form of accounts to be kept, whereas this was not so in other states. The question may well be raised whether direct regulation of accounts does not tend to make the prescribed methods the maximum of performance which is likely to result rather than the minimum from which the regulated companies should progress. Indeed, experience would indicate that this is the tendency which develops in practice.

Most, if not all, of the state public service commissions permitted, through the uniform system of accounts prescribed by them, the use of the so-called retirement reserve method [1] instead of service life depreciation allowances in respect of the operating properties of the utility companies. Years before, utility companies (particularly in the street railway days) had contended that there was no necessity for their setting up allowances for depreciation of property, as the renewals and replacements currently made were claimed to be a sufficient offset to wear and tear. Accruing obsolescence was blithely ignored. Public accountants urged on the utilities the need for recognizing accruing depreciation but with little success, and I well recall that back in the early 1900's our firm usually found it necessary to qualify its reports on the accounts of public utilities because we found no allowances made for depreciation and an unwillingness to recognize the need for them.

Unfortunately, the permission given by the public service

[1] Based on making allowances to provide for absorbing the cost of property retirements estimated to occur within a relatively short period of years. The effect was primarily to equalize the charges against annual operations

commissions, under their legal powers, to allow public utilities to use the so-called retirement reserve method brought about an accounting impasse. The accounting profession as a whole was, I believe, convinced that service life depreciation was a sound principle for the public utilities just as much as for industrial concerns. In the circumstances, however, there was nothing that accountants could do but assure themselves that full disclosure was made of the actual procedure and make their certificates subject to a reservation as to the adequacy of the retirement reserve.

The telephone companies were a notable exception to the utilities generally, and followed the service-life depreciation plan. I have heard some electrical utility operators say they wish now it had been the practice in their industry at a much earlier date to use the service-life depreciation plan rather than the retirement reserve method. It is unfortunate that the commissions did not use their influence and powers to secure the introduction years ago of the service-life plan. At that time it might have been done with less hardship than to make the change now.

Today the commissions are urging, or even requiring, the service-life depreciation method, but it seems to me they must also be practical about it and recognize that there must be a period of transition to permit of the change-over from one method to the other. There are too many problems of financial policy involved to permit of an overnight change. So far as annual depreciation allowances are concerned, many utilities are gradually bringing their former retirement allowances up to the amounts required for service-life depreciation purposes. To bring the accumulated allowances or reserves up to the full amount required, however, will take a considerable time for many of them. Equity requires that the

---

for the cost of property retirements, rather than to accumulate a reserve equal to that which would normally accrue under service life depreciation practice.

commissions recognize their concurrence in the use of the retirement reserve method over many years and that they should accordingly seek to work out the transition problem in a way that will impose the least hardship on the utilities and their security holders.

In 1936 the Federal Power Commission prescribed a new uniform system of accounts for the electrical utilities coming within its jurisdiction, and the National Association of Railways and Utilities Commissioners recommended a similar system which was adopted by many of the state utilities commissions. The most significant features of the new system of accounts are the stated requirement for service life depreciation practice in place of the former retirement reserve method, and the so-called "aboriginal cost" requirement that "all amounts included in the accounts for . . . plant acquired as an operating unit or system shall be stated at the original cost incurred by the person who first devoted the property to utility service," with supplemental accounts to record the differences between such original cost and the cost of the property to the present corporate owner.

The "aboriginal cost" requirement has led accountants to the conclusion that, if the studies necessary to determine "original cost" as defined by the Commission indicate it to be substantially less than corporate cost, which latter is the cost of the property to the present owner, disclosure of the difference is essential in the balance sheets of utilities which independent accountants may be called upon to certify.

Time does not permit of going into all the questions which arise out of this revolutionary concept of cost of property in a public utility enterprise. Some of them are (a) the disposition eventually to be made of the difference arising from the use of the two cost bases, (b) the segregation of the difference between tangible and intangible assets, and (c) the effect on the determination of depreciation allowances. This is in addition to the difficulty in many instances of getting at a dependable "original cost" of property which may have changed hands a number of times over a period of years, with varying methods of accounting for property costs in force during such period, particularly in the matter of such elements of cost as capitalizable interest and overhead, and with possibly incomplete or inadequate records available from predecessor owners in which case resort must be had to estimates of cost at time of the original acquisition.

Despite the fact that public utilities (other than railroads) are for the most part under just about as effective a control as the railroads through the various state commissions, the Federal Power Commission, and the Federal Communications Commission, which have jurisdiction in the case of the utilities, the development in respect of the examination of their financial statements and the certification thereof by independent public accountants has been different from that of the railroads. Today published statements of most utilities bear the certificate of independent public accountants. This development was already under way prior to the enactment of the Securities Act of 1933, but it received a further stimulus therefrom in that, whereas railroads are exempt from the provisions of that Act, other public utility companies are not, and are required by the Act to have their financial statements certified by independent public accountants when offering securities to the investing public.

A series of Federal laws were enacted from 1933 to 1940, all of which have important accounting and auditing implications. The first was the well-known Securities Act of 1933, which required registration (first with the Federal Trade Commission, and from 1934 on with the Securities and Exchange Commission) of securities to be offered to the public. Among its provisions which are both of interest and importance to the accountant are that a balance sheet and profit and loss statement of the issuer, which are to be included in the documents filed with the Commission, shall be "certified by an independent public or certified accountant"; that the balance sheet shall show "all of the assets of the issuer, the nature and cost thereof, whenever determinable, in such detail and in such form as the Commission shall prescribe (with intangible items segregated), including any loan in excess of $20,000 to any officer, director, stockholder, or person directly or indirectly controlling or controlled by the issuer, or person under direct or indirect common control with the issuer, and all the liabilities of the issuer in such detail and such form as the Commission shall prescribe, including surplus of the issuer showing how and from what sources such surplus was created . . ."; that a profit and loss statement for the three latest years, similarly certified, shall be filed which shall show "earnings and income, the nature and source thereof, and the expenses and fixed charges in such detail and such form as the Commission shall prescribe . . . ," and that "such statement shall show what the practice of the issuer has been . . . as to the character of the charges, dividends or other distributions made against its various surplus accounts, and as to depreciation, depletion, and maintenance charges, in such detail and form as the Commission shall prescribe, and if stock dividends or avails from the sale of rights have been credited to income, they shall be shown separately with the statement of the basis upon which the credit is computed, and such statement shall also differentiate between any recurring and nonrecurring income and between any investment and operating income."

Broad powers are given the Commission for the administration of the Act, some of which, as just indicated, touch on accounting questions. The liability of the auditor and of others participating in the registration for any untrue statements of material facts or omissions to state material facts required to be stated or necessary to make the statements in the registration statement not misleading has been the subject of much public attention and needs no detailed comment at this time.

The Securities Exchange Act, enacted in 1934, provided for the regulation of securities exchanges, for the registration of corporate securities listed thereon, and for the filing of annual reports with the Commission by corporations having such listed securities outstanding. The Securities and Exchange Commission, which was created by that act, was given broad administrative powers including some referring to accounting matters. Although the certification of financial statements included in such annual reports is not obligatory under the Act, the Commission was authorized to require it by regulation and it has promulgated such requirement.

Accountants have taken seriously the provisions of the two securities acts and have sought to impress the importance thereof on their clients as well, particularly in respect of those accounting matters which are particularly within the scope of the auditor's duties. The requirements of the acts and the activities of the Securities and Exchange Commission have given valuable support to accountants in their continuous efforts for improvements in accounting practice and for the adequacy of disclosures essential to presenting a complete picture of financial position and results of operations.

The Public Utility Act of 1935 with its rigorous control of public utility holding companies by the Securities and Exchange Commission contains further important accounting provisions. Among them is one "to prevent the payment of dividends out of capital or unearned surplus" excepting with the approval of the Commission. This distinction between earned and unearned surplus is of interest to the accountant because, although it has become a recognized distinction in accounting practice, corporate laws of but few states specifically provide for, or mention, such a distinction. Because of the absence of a statutory requirement for such a distinction, some lawyers have at times objected to its being made in the balance sheets of their clients.

Accountants generally, I believe, feel that, as expressed on occasion by both the Securities and Exchange Commission and the New York Stock Exchange, the omission from the corporate law of a state of a requirement for what would otherwise be regarded as good accounting practice does not justify a failure to apply such accounting practice or principle by a corporation incorporated in such state. In other words, accepted accounting principles have a validity which does not necessarily arise out of specific enunciation or sanction of law.

By amendments to the Federal Power Act made in 1935, the Federal Power Commission is now empowered to "ascertain and determine, and by order fix the proper and adequate rates of depreciation of the several classes of property of each . . . public utility." It is further provided that ". . . public utilities subject to the jurisdiction of the Commission shall not charge to operating expenses any depreciation charges on classes of property other than those prescribed by the Commission, or charge with respect to any class of property a percentage of depreciation other than that prescribed therefor by the Commission." Still further, "no . . . public utility shall in any case include in any form under its operating or other expenses any depreciation or other charge or expenditure included elsewhere as a depreciation charge or otherwise under its operating or other expenses."

In theory at least, the auditor might find himself in an embarrassing situation if it appeared that the Commission had decreed an unduly low or unduly high rate of depreciation on public utility property, and the company is not permitted under the Act to set up its depreciation allowance at any different amount from that prescribed by the Commission, regardless of how completely the opinion of managers or officers might agree with the view of the auditor. In such a case, apparently, the only recourse of the auditor would be to qualify his report and to indicate whether, in his opinion, the prescribed allowance is inadequate or excessive. Since at best the computation of depreciation allowances is to a considerable extent a matter of estimate, however, and since it is to be presumed that the Commission will wish to have the depreciation allowances as nearly as may be in accord with what all concerned believe to be the proper allowance, it seems unlikely that many, if any, situations of this kind are likely to arise in practice. There is always the danger, however, that expediency may influence a regulatory body when it is making a decision in a particular case. Mr. George O. May effectively pointed out in the February, 1941, *Journal of Accountancy* the need for avoiding any departure from sound accounting principles on the ground of expediency.[1]

The Trust Indenture Act of 1939 (enacted as an amendment of the Securities Act of 1933) imposes various obligations on the issuer of securities coming within the scope of the Act, including the requirement that in the case of conditions precedent, compliance with which is subject to verification by accountants (such as preservation of specified ratios, amount of net quick assets, negative-pledge clauses, and other similar specific conditions), a certificate or opinion of an independent public accountant is to be furnished. The Act prescribes the following recitals as the basis of any certificate or opinion so issued:

> Each certificate or opinion with respect to compliance with a condition or covenant provided for in the indenture shall include (1) a statement that the person making such certificate or opinion has read such covenant or condition; (2) a brief statement as to the nature and scope of the examination or investigation upon which the statements or opinions contained in such certificate or opinion are based; (3) a statement

[1] Vol. LXXI, No. 2, "Accounting Principles and Regulatory Expediency," pp. 116–118.

that, in the opinion of such person, he has made such examination or investigation as is necessary to enable him to express an informed opinion as to whether or not such covenant or condition has been complied with; and (4) a statement as to whether or not, in the opinion of such person, such condition or covenant has been complied with.

The Investment Company Act of 1940 grew out of the study which the Securities and Exchange Commission had been directed by the Public Utility Act of 1935 to make of "the functions and activities of investment trusts and investment companies, the corporate structures, and investment policies of such trusts and companies, and the influence exerted by such trusts . . . upon . . . investment policies."

So-called investment trusts had been a relatively small factor in the American financial picture until the late 1920's when they had a mushroom growth with a widespread participation by the public. The prices at which the securities of such trusts were issued, or to which they quickly rose, went even beyond the inflated prices of securities generally, and approached the dimensions of the "South Sea Bubble" in England some two hundred years before.

After the crash in the stock market in 1929 the prices of investment trust stocks generally nose-dived as rapidly and drastically as they had previously risen. The Commission as a result of its study was of the opinion that there had been various abuses by those who dominated the companies and that protective measures were desirable. In contradistinction to much of the other New Deal legislation, the Commission and representatives of the investment companies were able to agree on the legislation to be enacted.

Representatives of the American Institute of Accountants appeared before the Senate Committee having the bill in charge and also conferred with the Commission so that when the bill came out of committee it contained provisions in respect of the reports to be filed with the Commission by the investment companies and of the examinations of the financial statements to be made by independent public accountants which met in a large measure the views of the accounting profession.

Under the Investment Company Act, not only financial statements in reports filed with the Commission, but also those in reports required to be transmitted to stockholders, must if required by the Commission be certified by independent public accountants. The Act deals in some detail with the accountant's certificate, as indicated by the following provision:

> The certificate of such independent public accountants shall be based upon an audit not less in scope or procedures followed than that which independent public accountants would ordinarily make for the purpose of presenting comprehensive and dependable financial statements, and shall contain such information as the Commission may prescribe, by rules and regulations in the public interest or for the protection of investors, as to the nature and scope of the audit and the findings and opinion of the accountants. Each such report shall state that such independent public accountants have verified securities owned, either by actual examination, or by receipt of a certificate from the custodian, as the Commission may prescribe by rules and regulations.

The concluding sentence, embodying a statutory requirement for an explicit statement regarding the verification of securities owned by the investment trust or company, is to be noted.

An earlier development than any of those regulatory enactments already referred to, which has had some influence on accounting but which, because of its timing, has had the effect of rather limiting the contact of the public accountant with its particular field, is that of statutory bank examinations.

At the time that the Federal Government first instituted, through the Comptroller of the Currency, a system of national bank examinations, and the banking departments of the different states instituted periodical examinations of state banks and trust companies, the profession of public accountancy in the United States was hardly born. Indeed, if there were any men then practicing as public accountants, they were only a scattered few and none of them would have had a staff capable of examining even a moderate-sized bank. The consequence was that the periodical examination of banks was undertaken by the governmental authorities above-mentioned instead of public accountants being retained, as has been the general practice in England and Canada.

The much earlier development of the profession in England caused it to be called upon to undertake bank examinations when the need for them became evident in England. Consequently, the professional accountant has continued through the years to include the examination of the accounts and assets of banks among his activities in both England and Canada, with a supervisory relationship by the governmental authorities which does not include periodical examinations unless there seems to be special reason therefor.

Some banks retain accountants to assist the examining committees of their boards of directors. At the present time, however, the auditing of banks by professional accountants is not widespread, many banks considering the statutory examinations as sufficient.

Similarly, in the case of insurance companies, when state supervision of the companies, including an examination of their accounts and assets from time to time, came into being, it was undertaken by the commissioners or departments in various states because there was no public accounting profession [1] of either scope or standing which could undertake the periodical examination and the certification of the published reports, and thus permit the supervision by the governmental bodies to be devoted to phases of regulation other

[1] The State of New Hampshire in 1851 created a commission of three to make annual examinations of insurance companies, and the Commonwealth of Massachusetts in 1858 provided that "it shall be the duty of said commission to visit and examine whenever they shall deem necessary any insurance company."

than the examination of the accounts of the insurance companies. It is of interest, however, that a number of large life insurance companies have published statements certified by independent public accountants ever since the Hughes investigation in 1905, and that a considerable increase in the number of companies issuing certified statements in their annual reports has occurred in recent years.

It may be noted in passing that accounting for both banks and insurance companies lagged behind the development of accounting for industrial and mercantile enterprises. Published bank statements for many years were rather crude and could hardly be said to have measured up to the requirements of disclosure of all material information such as they expected to find in the statements required of their borrowers. It has been only in recent years, for instance, that notations have appeared on bank statements of the investments which are pledged to secure certain types of deposits or in respect of fiduciary powers, and only comparatively recently that any substantial number of banking institutions have published an income statement.

The accounting of insurance companies, particularly of life companies, has continued largely unchanged for many years, and their accounting methods and the statutory form of statements submitted to their policyholders are still rather primitive in some respects. The April, 1941, *Journal of Accountancy* contained an article by Mr. Charles E. Mather on "The Income Statement of Life Insurance Company" [1] which is stated to be based on the auditor's conviction that life insurance companies should provide their policyholders with reports at least as informative as those issued by the average commercial corporation to its stockholders. He suggests that the usual balance sheet should be supplemented by a new form of income statement (presented in the article) in place of the "rather cryptic" statement now customary.

[1] Vol. LXXI, No. 4, pp. 322–333.

Social Uses of Accounting

In an *Encyclopaedia Britannica* article on Money it was pointed out that money has come to include anything that performs the work of money; that the most important function of money is that of facilitating exchange; that the earliest economic writers saw plainly that division of employments was only possible through the agency of a medium of exchange, and that a second function of money is that of affording a ready means for estimating the comparative values of different commodities.

Not only does money talk but money symbols are one means of expressing various phases of our modern civilization, including its social conditions and development. With the widespread ownership not only of our large corporations but of many of medium size as well, and with the public today having investments in every phase of business, industrial, mercantile, public utility, and so on, published financial statements have assumed ever-increasing importance. Such statements are indicative of the success or failure of individual enterprises and a reflection, in a broad way, of the business of the country as a whole.

With the recognition that in our modern society capital, labor, and the consumer all have an interest in the national economy, and consequently in the success of business and in the distribution of its produce, the financial statements of business concerns obviously have a social interest. The dependability of the representations contained in such statements by reason of the opinion of the accountant expressed thereon — in the terminology of the man in the street, "certified" — makes the accountant, in a sense, a party to such uses as financial statements may properly have in the consideration of social questions and their attempted solution.

I cannot help feeling that, with the pendulum having apparently swung to an extreme in the present state of labor relations (as evidenced by numerous strikes which appear to be seriously slowing down the defense program), the time must come when disputes between capital and labor, in so far as they relate to wage rates and the division of the avails of production effort between those who contribute capital and those who contribute labor, respectively, to what in effect is a joint enterprise, must rest for their solution in no small measure on what financial statements disclose concerning the operations of the business. The balance sheet and income account, which may normally suffice for the purpose of stockholders who should be informed from time to time of the financial status and operating progress of an enterprise, will need to be supplemented in negotiations or arbitrations between capital and labor with more detailed data pertinent to the questions at issue. Nevertheless, these basic financial statements with the support of examination and certification by independent accountants are a starting point for the analyses required to afford the data necessary to permit the negotiating parties or arbitrators to come to conclusions equitable to both sides.

As between capital and consumer, what is indicated in the paragraph immediately preceding has been in use for years past in rate proceedings relating to railroads and other utility corporations. There is there involved, of course, the special factor of monopoly, partial or complete, with the necessity of determining fair charges for service on the basis of not merely "what the traffic will bear" but also of what should be regarded as the limit of a fair return on the capital employed in such an enterprise. To be sure, proceedings of this kind under the past decisions of the United States Supreme Court have, in respect of the capital employed, had to take into account factors other than those shown directly in the financial statements. For instance, the amount allowed for property employed in the operations of a utility is not usually confined to its cost (either new or depreciated), but such cost is considered as one of the elements in arriving at the fair value of the property at the time reasonable rates are being set.

It has been stated that when, some forty odd years ago, in *Smyth* v. *Ames*, the United States Supreme Court held that present fair value, rather than original cost, was to be the substance of the rate base, those who were seeking to have railroad rates reduced apparently felt they had obtained a victory in the public interest. During the years leading up to that decision the price level had been, broadly speaking, tending downward. Today, after a period during which the price level had risen greatly, the prudent investment theory has been strongly advocated by those seeking to have rates for electric light and power and other forms of public service reduced. The prudent investment theory, as expressed by the Massachusetts Public Service Commission in the *Middlesex and Boston Rate Case* (1914), is that "capital honestly and prudently invested must, under normal conditions, be taken as the controlling factor in fixing the basis for computing fair and reasonable rates; that if there is mismanagement causing loss, such loss must be charged against the stockholders legally responsible for the mismanagement; . . ."[1]

In a brief filed by the Attorney General of the United States as *amicus curiae* in a case then pending before the Supreme Court, he defined "prudent investment" as "the amount reasonably and honestly invested in public utility properties used and useful in the public service." Also, in arguing for abandonment of the fair value rule for rate-making purposes, he said, "the rule of prudent investment, combining as it does exactness, ease of application and a proper principle for the determination of just compensation, is the standard for rate making best adapted to modern busi-

[1] 2 Ann. Rep. Mass. P. S. C. 99.

ness conditions and practice in this country." [1] Apparently, the Attorney General would make it possible to use the books of account more directly and with less adjustment of the figures shown therein than has been the case in rate determinations based on the fair value theory. The question may well be raised whether he is not oversimplifying the problem of rate making when in expressing his preference for the prudent investment theory he includes among its advantages "exactness" and "ease of application." Rate making, if it is to be fair to all the interests concerned, will always present a complex situation, and exactness and ease of application are not likely to be found inherent in the use of the prudent investment theory. At best it is a question of relativity of ease of determination under the respective theories of fair value and of prudent investment. If the prudent investment theory is to be adopted in place of the fair value theory — and for purposes of the present discussion I express no opinion in favor of one or the other — it should be based on more fundamental considerations than fancied "exactness" and "ease of application."

A further development since the enunciation of the prudent investment theory in the Massachusetts case above cited is the present requirement of the Federal Power Commission, the Federal Communications Commission, and the utility commissions of various states that utility property accounts shall be so segregated that they will show the original cost thereof to the person who first devoted such property to public use, and separately any amount by which the cost to the present owner exceeds such original cost.

To the extent that fixed assets may now appear on the books of operating utilities at more than their cost to the present owners merely by reason of their having been written up because of assumed appreciation in value, I think little,

[1] *Denis J. Driscoll, Thomas C. Buchanan and Richard J. Beamish, et al.* v. *Edison Light & Power Company*, 307 U.S. 104 (1939).

if any, argument would be offered by accountants for recognizing such written-up values. Where, however, the properties appear on the books of the owning corporations at actual cost to them as contrasted with a lesser cost to the predecessor owner, the question of whether such predecessor cost is proper for rate-making purposes is still to be passed upon by the Supreme Court.

In the Supreme Court's opinion in the case of *American Telephone & Telegraph Co. et al.* v. *U. S. A. et al.* (1936), which sustained the right of the Federal Communications Commission to require property accounts to be set up on the original cost basis, the Court, while expressing no opinion on the manner in which such accounts should enter into any rate determinations, made it clear that both for purposes of reflecting the accounting company's assets and for computing depreciation allowances any excess of legitimate corporate investment over cost to the original owner would continue to be recognized as a part of the property investment. For such use, however, as the public interest may warrant, the information afforded by property accounts kept on the original cost basis will be available.

Another direction in which accounts may serve a social use is indicated by the recommendation in the 1940 annual report of the Comptroller of the Currency that he "be authorized, in his discretion, to forbid a national bank to declare or pay dividends on its capital stock until there has been satisfactory compliance with his requirements." He points out that "responsibility for the legality and propriety of each dividend should continue to rest upon the board of directors of the particular bank as at present, except where it affirmatively appears to the Comptroller that the declaration of a dividend should not be permitted because of the existence of violations of law or unsafe or unsound banking practices which, if continued, would endanger the safety of the bank and its depositors."

Senator Glass has introduced a bill in the Senate which, among other provisions, would make it unlawful for any insured bank to declare or pay any dividend on any of its capital stock when the Comptroller of the Currency (as to national banks) or the Board of Directors of the Federal Deposit Insurance Corporation (as to insured state banks) object thereto as being in the opinion of the Comptroller or Board, respectively, not "compatible with the best interests of such bank, its depositors or other creditors, or with the public interest."

Obviously, the accounts of the bank and the examination thereof would be a primary source of the data needed by the Comptroller or the Board in determining whether a proposed dividend would be undesirable in the circumstances of a given bank.

The foregoing examples of areas in which public authorities have assumed accounting or auditing responsibilities, or have exercised controls in those areas, will serve to indicate that the functions and responsibilities of the public accountant as auditor have been both increased and more sharply defined as the years have gone on.

II. PRESENT-DAY AUDITING PRACTICE

WHERE THE purpose of an audit is to enable the auditor to express an opinion upon the balance sheet and the related income and surplus statements, he will seek to establish by such internal and external evidence as may prove available the propriety of the amounts at which the various assets appearing on the balance sheet are stated, the amounts of the liabilities which should appear on the balance sheet (either direct liabilities which should be definitely included or contingent liabilities which should be noted thereon), the amount and description of the capital stock (or other form of capital as in the case of partnerships), and the amount of surplus (with proper classification, if required, between capital surplus and earned surplus and indication of any restriction on the distribution of the surplus, whether contractual or through such action as the reacquisition of the company's own stock and the holding of it uncanceled in its treasury).

The internal evidence in support of the financial statements may be said to include the records themselves from which the statements have been prepared, their coherence, various records tying in with one another, the subsidiary books being in balance with their respective controlling accounts, and the existence of a system of internal control and check which appears to be reasonably adapted to the circumstances under which the client concern operates and which appears to be satisfactorily functioning.

The external evidence may be briefly described as documents which originate outside the client's office, and particularly statements and confirmations which come directly to the auditor from outside sources. It may also be said to consist of the assets themselves which can be the subject of objective inspection, as distinguished from the record of ownership thereof, as, for example, stocks and bonds or notes receivable.

The existence of a system of internal check and control and the effectiveness or otherwise with which it appears to be functioning have been emphasized more and more in recent years as an important consideration in determining the scope and extent of sampling and testing in making an audit. Consequently it follows that the system of internal check and control must be the subject of observation and testing, both in an initial audit and by way of review as to changes for better or worse during succeeding audits.

Alertness by the auditor to every indication which he may gain from the nature and treatment of transactions which come under his review is indispensable in an effective audit. The most painstaking inquiry into the existing system is no substitute for alertness and imagination.

It may be observed, too, that an "over-all" impression of the organization and personnel of the business and its functioning is helpful, and may sometimes be even more significant than the apparent plan or system of internal check and control and its intended functioning. Such an over-all impression is something like the doctor's impression of his patient's appearance and progress, or loss of ground, as distinguished from the technical details or symptoms recorded on chart or questionnaire.

Accounting Evidence

In speaking of accounting evidence the auditor may be visualized as acting somewhat in the capacity of a judge or jury who considers the evidence submitted in support of the representations made in the financial statements or, going one step farther, in supporting or corroborating the entries made in the books of account from which the statements have been prepared. Just as in the case of a judge or jury, the purpose of the consideration of the evidence is that a conclusion may be reached as to the dependability or otherwise of the representations contained in the statements and an opinion be expressed accordingly.

Two important distinctions come to mind, however, between the position of the judge or jury and that of the auditor. One distinction is that a judge or jury has the evidence brought to it by parties in interest who are presenting their case for consideration. This is true only in part in the case of the auditor. For the most part he must search for the evidence, and to a considerable extent he must determine what evidence shall be presented to him.

Another distinction is that, of the evidence brought to judge or jury, some of it is not infrequently excluded on the ground that it is irrelevant, incompetent, or otherwise not acceptable under applicable legal rules of evidence. The auditor, however, is not so limited. Whatever evidence is before him may and should be considered for its informative and probative value. Some of it may have very little value, but even in such cases the possibility of helpful suggestion is not to be overlooked.

It follows that the type of evidence which comes before the auditor is frequently less conclusive than would be required in a court of law. However, he must consider it for what it may be worth and exercise his best judgment regarding its acceptability. The auditor is not bound by any rules of evidence in conducting his examination and, on the contrary, any effort to withhold any evidence from his consideration should ordinarily lead him to insist upon its submission.

The books from which the statements have been prepared are themselves part of the accounting evidence. They are presumed to be a record made approximately at the time the transactions occurred, and therefore are *prima facie* to be accepted as evidence to the extent that they are not contradicted by other more conclusive evidence of the actual nature of the transactions which they purport to reflect. Entries therein may on occasion, however, because of the absence of supporting evidence which should be available, be questioned until substantiated to the auditor's satisfaction.

Other accounting evidence includes any relevant documents which may throw light upon, or corroborate the truthfulness and correctness of, the entries in the books, or may yield information concerning contingent liabilities or other matters which have not yet become the subject of closed transactions and which may, therefore, merely be noted on the balance sheet or income statement or in the explanatory notes appended thereto instead of being recorded in the principal books of account. Among such documents may be mentioned bank statements, paid checks and notes, copies of deposit tickets, petty cash vouchers, invoices for materials or other merchandise purchased or for expenses incurred, pay rolls, cost records, copies of bills rendered to customers, approved debit and credit memoranda relating to adjustments of customers' or suppliers' accounts, construction authorizations, engineers' reports, leases and other contracts, minute books, correspondence relating to unusual transactions, inventories, computations of depletion and depreciation allowances, and so on.

Sometimes the evidence relating to certain transactions is largely or wholly oral, that is, explanations from officers or others who know the facts regarding transactions for which entries have been made but for which little or no documentary evidence is available. Obviously, oral evidence, in the form of explanations, is not to be disregarded by the auditor, though naturally the acceptability of the evidence so received may involve the exercise of even more judgment than when the evidence is in documentary form.

A considerable part of the practical work of the auditor is to test the dependability of the books of account by comparison of the accounting evidence with the entries to which it relates. The extent to which such evidence shall be accepted as conclusive is one of the elements in the work of the auditor that make it professional in character since it involves the exercise of judgment and educated opinion.

Since it is not practicable in the case of any but small concerns to examine all the transactions of the period which has elapsed since the last preceding examination, a second exercise of judgment relating to the evidence is the extent to which it shall be reviewed and compared with the book entries. This is no easy matter and, indeed, thinking and the exercising of judgment are usually not easy. Thomas A. Edison is reputed to have said that there is no extreme to which a man will not go in the effort to escape the labor of thinking.

The need for making such a judgment, however, cannot be evaded. It goes without saying that the greater the experience of the auditor the better the basis for his judgment, and the greater the assurance with which he comes to a conclusion about the extent to which, in a given case, his testing and sampling or, as it might also be described, the use to be made of the accounting evidence shall be carried.

Clients' Written Representations Regarding Inventories, Liabilities, and Other Matters

A development of more recent years, which may be regarded as in the nature of supplementary accounting evidence, is that of having responsible officers or other representatives of the client in positions of authority give to the auditor an "inventory certificate" and a "liability certificate." The purpose of the former is to have someone make a definite statement to the auditor, on behalf of the client, that the inventory of a stated amount (perhaps divided into a few broad classes) has been taken under the direction of the signer of the certificate; that to the best of his knowledge and belief quantities are correct and were determined by actual count, weight, or measurement; that the entire inventory is the unencumbered property of the client, has not been pledged as collateral, and includes no items billed by the company prior to the balance sheet date or held on consignment; that the inventory is priced at cost or market, whichever is lower, and is not in excess of net realizable value; that the basis of pricing and method of computation is the same as was used at the end of the previous fiscal period and that the general basis on which cost is determined is as described (as first-in, first-out; average; last-in, first-out, etc.); that no obsolete, damaged, or unusable materials or merchandise are included in the inventory in excess of net realizable value; and that the amount stated is a fair and proper valuation of the inventory.

The liability certificate is a statement or representation that, to the best of the knowledge and belief of the signer, all liabilities have been taken up on the books of account as at the balance sheet date, including liability for all merchandise shipped and billed to the client prior to that date; that none of the assets of the company was, or is now, pledged or hypothecated as security for any liabilities except as disclosed in the certificate; and that, excepting for those indicated in the liability certificate, there were no contingent liabilities, no purchase commitments for the purchase of materials or supplies at prices in excess of the prevailing market prices, or repurchase agreements for merchandise previously sold, no other commitments, contracts, or leases which might adversely affect the company, and no unused balance of letters of credit outstanding at the balance sheet date. Further, the liability certificate should contain a statement of the approximate amount of any contractual obligations for plant construction, purchase of real property, equipment, and rights; a statement that there were no subordinations of liabilities at the balance sheet date, and that between that date and the signing of the certificate there has been no material change in respect of contingent liabilities, commitments, etc., except as indicated in the certificate.

The securing of such certificates has become widely recognized in the profession as an essential part of auditing procedure so that there may be no question of the client's having made a definite representation, on the one hand, of the propriety of the inventory taking and valuation and, on the other, of the liabilities, including those of a contingent character, which the client either knows or should know about. Naturally, such certificates must not be relied upon as substitutes for but as supplementary to inquiry by the auditor into the various items mentioned. The very request for these certificates, however, has the effect of facing the client squarely with the basis on which the inventory has been, or should have been, taken, and of perhaps having the client bring to the attention of the auditor information concerning those types of liabilities which are not necessarily recorded on the books of account, such as various classes of contingent liabilities, merchandise and construction commitments, and other contractual obligations, hypothecation of assets, etc. Also, it may lead to a disclosure of direct liabilities which have not been reflected on the books before their closing.

Some auditors go so far as to require comprehensive written representations by executives of the client in respect of various phases of property accounting, reserves for depreciation and depletion, and the validity of the accounts and notes receivable, as well as some other special features. This is not a general practice, though some extension of the request for clients' written representations regarding the property accounting may at times be helpful. Retirements of fixed assets are not always reported to the accounting department, and a request for the signature of a superintendent or plant manager to a certificate that all sales, dismantlements, and abandonments of plant and equipment during the period of audit have been reported might cause him to recall retirements which had not been reported. Engineers have not infrequently found that when an inventory is taken of fixed assets a portion of those carried on the books is found to be missing, apparently because of failure on the part of those responsible for reporting retirements to the accounting departments. Where there seems reason for requesting such a certificate from an operating official, the logical corollary certificate would be by the controller or other accounting officer that all reported sales, dismantlements, and abandonments of plant items reported to his department had been properly recorded.

Developments in Auditing Procedure

Some illustrations of present-day auditing procedures which reflect the application of what has been learned from the auditor's experience through the years are as follows:

(a) Review of the composition of the surplus balance and of the consideration for which capital stock and other securities were issued is now considered an essential part of the auditor's duties. The procedures in this respect would now also include a review of minutes of stockholders' and directors' meetings at organization and for significant matters in subsequent years, the certificate of incorporation, and any changes in capital stock issues since organization. More attention is now being paid on the occasion of an initial audit to establishing the basis of fixed assets, unless other public accountants have satisfactorily covered the ground in prior examinations. This may involve a general review of the fixed asset accounts from the date of organization of the company. In earlier years when the property account frequently had its inception merely as an offset to the face value of securities issued, that account was more or less accepted "as is," and the auditor was frequently content to accept the balance of property accounts at the opening of the year for which he made his initial audit, without attempting to establish the basis of the amount at which the fixed assets were carried.

(b) Many accountants now feel that a second or cut-off bank reconciliation is a desirable part of auditing procedures in respect of cash. This procedure is a development during the past decade. It was adopted as a means of ascertaining whether any checks were outstanding when the first reconciliation was made but improperly excluded therefrom, and of detecting other possible irregularities which might more readily be brought to light by a second cut-off without notice than at a regular reconciliation date. There may be cases in which for special reasons it is impracticable or unreasonable to resort to the second reconciliation plan. If such be the case, the principal objectives of the second reconciliation may be attained by obtaining bank statements and paid checks at a date following the first reconciliation, and (1) seeing whether any checks included therein were apparently issued in the preceding period but were not listed as outstanding in the first reconciliation, (2) comparing such outstanding items with the returned paid checks so far as they may have been paid by the bank, (3) noting that deposits in transit over the first reconciliation date were promptly credited in the subsequent bank statement, and (4) learning of any charge-backs of deposited items.

(c) Another procedure now generally followed is to obtain duplicate bank deposit slips from the bank (or to have the bank authenticate for the auditor copies prepared from the client's records), usually for a short period, and to compare the detail of the items shown thereon with the source of postings to customers' and other accounts. Perhaps the warning should be given that since, in those banks where the block system is used, the tellers do not compare the items making up the deposit in detail with the deposit slips at the time originally received, the value of this check is in such cases not so conclusive as might be wished. Even in such circumstances, however, it has some value. An effective method which may be used when it is practicable for the auditor to be present at the client's office during a period is for the auditor to make such comparisons immediately after the cashier has made up his deposit, and to see that such deposit is transmitted to the bank without further access thereto by the cashier.

(d) Auditors now endeavor, in all cases where practicable, to obtain outside direct confirmation of balance sheet items. In addition to asking banks to confirm independently the balances on deposit at the balance sheet date, the banks are asked to confirm direct or contingent liabilities of the client which may be known to them, endorsements, collateral held, items held for collection, etc. Collection agencies are also asked to confirm notes or acceptances held by them. Legal counsel is asked for information regarding suits or other liabilities known to them. Life insurance companies are asked for computations of cash surrender value of life insurance policies which may be held. Consignees or consignors of merchandise are requested to confirm balances shown by the client's records. Trustees of bond issues, registrars and transfer agents of capital stock issues, and sometimes the secretary or other pertinent official of the state of incorporation are asked for information which they can supply for the confirmation of security amounts shown by the client's records. Deposits held by such organizations as transportation lines, custom brokers, and public utilities are also confirmed directly with the holders.

(e) Improvement in plant accounting records which accountants have been urging for many years has been effected by many corporations. When this has been done, such records permit the auditor to review more intelligently the changes in fixed asset accounts. This is particularly true when a work order or work authorization plan for the accounting pertaining to plant changes is in use.

(f) Auditors pay more attention today than in earlier years to a review of the client's files of contracts or agreements as a source of information concerning possible liabilities, such as service or operating agreements, officers' and employees' bonus agreements, pension plans, purchase agreements, etc.

(g) While not a generally accepted procedure, circularization of creditors is not infrequently resorted to, especially if a review of the internal procedures for recording creditors' invoices indicates them to be unsatisfactory.

Extensions of Auditing Procedure

Over the years during which I have been observing the development of auditing procedure I have seen it continuously extended. For instance, I recall that forty years ago when we were verifying bank balances we usually relied upon the bank passbook, which was balanced by the bank upon request of the depositor, for the amount of the balance standing to the credit of the depositor. Confirmation of deposit balances by banks directly to the accountant was in its infancy and not yet generally resorted to. Monthly bank statements, which had their origin in the Middle West, were just beginning to be heard of in the East. As a result of the development in respect of this item on the balance sheet, every effort is made today to obtain the assurance which comes from confirmation of bank balances directly to the auditor, by verification on the part of the bank of duplicate deposit tickets when details of cash receipts are being traced, by confirmation of notes payable or any other obligations of the client held by the bank, and of drafts, notes, or similar items held for collection.

In respect of two other important assets, usually classed as current on the balance sheet, there has been a marked development of auditing procedure through the years and a definite extension thereof as normal procedure where it is practicable and reasonable in the circumstances of the particular engagement. These two items are inventories and receivables.

Broadly speaking, there were for years in this country two schools of thought in respect of contact of the auditor with inventories of goods on hand. One school held to the thought of the much older profession in Britain where the auditor had not sought to establish physical contact with inventories except, presumably, in abnormal cases. It felt that the work of the auditor, since he is not to be considered an expert in materials or a valuer, should be confined to such evidence as the inventories (vouched for by those who were responsible for the stocktaking), financial books, stock records, and related documents, together with inquiry into the method of stock-taking and making accounting tests and checks of the inventories and supporting records.

Another school of thought, however, held that we should not be content with the practice and experience of the past but should seek to establish by physical contact with the inventory, through observation of the methods by which it is taken and by test inspection of quantities where this be practicable, the probable correctness of the inventory quantities. Some accountants had reached the point where they had been able to persuade many of their clients to assent to the inclusion of such physical contact with inventories in the scope of the auditor's examination. It was recognized, however, that this had not yet become a general practice in the profession, and could not therefore be regarded as normal procedure which could be expected to be followed in the absence of unusual circumstances indicating express need for such procedure.

The special committee appointed by the American Institute of Accountants in 1939 to consider possible extensions of auditing procedure adopted the view of the second school of thought and made the following recommendations regarding auditing procedures in respect of inventories:

(A) That hereafter, where the independent certified public accountant intends to report over his signature on the financial statements of a concern in which inventories are a material factor, it should be generally accepted auditing procedure that, in addition to making auditing tests and checks of the inventory accounts and records, he shall, wherever practicable and reasonable, be present, either in person or by his representatives, at the inventory taking and by suitable observation and inquiry satisfy himself as to the effectiveness of the methods of inventory taking and as to the measure of reliance which may be placed upon the client's representations as to inventories and upon the records thereof. In this connection the independent certified public accountant may require physical tests of inventories to be made under his observation.

In cases where the inventory is determined solely by means of a physical inventory at the end of the accounting period (or at a date prior or subsequent thereto but within a reasonable time thereof, with adequate records supporting the interim changes), it will ordinarily be necessary for the foregoing procedures to be followed at that time.

In cases where the concern maintains well kept and controlled perpetual inventory records supported by (1) a complete physical inventory at a date not coincident with the balance-sheet date, or (2) physical inventories of individual items taken from time to time so that the quantity of each item on hand is compared with the inventory record for that item at least once in each year, it will be satisfactory to undertake the procedure outlined at any interim date or dates selected by the auditor, his purpose being to satisfy himself as to the credibility of the perpetual inventory records and whether they may be relied upon to support the inventory totals as shown on the balance-sheet.

(B) That hereafter, in the case of inventories which in the ordinary course of business are in the hands of public warehouses or other outside custodians, direct confirmation in writing from such custodians is acceptable procedure; except that, where the amount involved represents a significant proportion of the current assets or of the total assets of a concern, the independent certified public accountant shall make supplementary inquiries.

The committee, however, took the precaution of accompanying its recommendations with the following warning:

It should be clearly understood that in undertaking these auditing procedures regarding inventories, the independent certified public accountant does so for the purpose of satisfying himself as to the credibility of the representations of the management regarding quantity and condition and does not hold himself out as a general appraiser, valuer, or expert in materials.

The recommendation of the committee in respect of physical tests of inventory was "viewed with alarm" by the profession in Great Britain and Canada. If an editorial in *The Accountant* [London] of June 24, 1939, written soon after the approval of the report submitted by the Committee to the Council of the American Institute at its May, 1939, meeting, may be regarded as indicative of the reaction of the profession generally in Britain, the extended auditing procedure in respect of inventories now to be regarded as normal procedure in this country is not likely to be adopted by our professional brethren across the sea, at least for some time to come.

An editorial in *The Canadian Chartered Accountant* of August, 1939, indicated a feeling probably akin to that expressed in *The Accountant* on the part of the profession in Canada.

The situation in respect of the circularization of receivables was somewhat different from that relating to physical contact with inventories. The same questions raised in respect of inventories, namely, that the auditor lacked the training for distinguishing between different qualities of even such relatively common materials as, for instance, steel, or of even recognizing commodities or products of various kinds in such fields as the chemical industry, did not for the most part obtain in respect of establishing the authenticity of the notes and accounts receivable by communication with the debtors.

In at least one line of business, that is, stock and commodity brokers, the confirmation practice had been an accepted procedure for many years past, and an audit would not have been considered complete or satisfactory if the auditor had not, through such communication with customers, had the opportunity to ascertain whether, upon being independently informed through statements of account from the client mailed under the control of the auditor, they took exception to the correctness of the balances standing to their debit or credit, or of the securities shown in such accounts as long or short, or of the commodity commitments indicated thereon.

In the industrial and mercantile fields the practice had been used to some extent, particularly where the system of internal check and control did not appear to be effective, or where the receivables consisted of a relatively few accounts of exceptionally large amount. Although the confirmation practice was gradually coming into greater use, it certainly could not be said up to 1939 that it was an essential auditing procedure in the absence of which the auditor would not give an unqualified certificate.

Practical problems were seen in making even a small test of the receivables of certain types of concerns, such as department stores and furniture instalment houses, automobile finance companies and small loan companies, milk companies and others in the field of house-to-house distribution, and the larger public utilities, where there may be in the case of one company anywhere from tens of thousands up to even a million or more accounts or notes receivable. In many of these cases the average receivable would be small, and both the type of many of the customers and the relativity of small individual accounts to the aggregate of the receivables would call for an undue amount of time from the auditor for the confirmation procedure with a consequent expense to the client which might well be disproportionate to any conceivable value of the results to be obtained.

In the case of at least one class of concerns, namely, the public utilities, it was seen that there is a factor of control of receivables which is additional to that of accounting check and control, namely, the cutting off of service in the event the consumer does not live up to the prescribed terms of payment, and his inability to get service elsewhere in the event of such termination of service. This gives a still greater assurance to the dependability of utility receivables for the purpose of the auditor's review of them. This service control factor, combined with the small balance for the average consumer, leads me to the conclusion that in the case of a utility with a large number of consumers and with a well-organized system of consumer accounting and internal check and control, confirmation of any but the smallest percentage of consumers' receivables is, if not quite impracticable, certainly unreasonable.

The recommendation of the committee was as follows:

> That hereafter, wherever practicable and reasonable, and where the aggregate amount of notes and accounts receivable represents a significant proportion of the current assets or of the total assets of a concern, confirmation of notes and accounts receivable by direct communication with the debtors shall be regarded as generally accepted auditing procedure in the examination of the accounts of a concern whose financial statements are accompanied by an independent certified public accountant's report; and that the method, extent, and time of confirming receivables in each engagement, and whether of all receivables or a part thereof, be determined by the independent certified public accountant as in other phases of procedure requiring the exercise of his judgment.

The Institute's Committee on Auditing Procedure has since issued a statement that,

> in the case of the receivables of department stores, instalment houses, chain stores, and other retailers, there might be question as to the reasonableness of applying the positive form of confirmation, but it is believed that there is no question as to the practicability and reasonableness of applying the negative form of confirmation which requires no reply unless the recipient challenges the balance shown. When dealing with housewives, as is the case in department stores particularly, the negative form is more practicable than the positive, as it places the recipient definitely on notice that the creditor's books show a stated balance, and that the auditor assumes the correctness of that balance unless the debtor objects within reasonable time.

In audits generally the so-called negative form is, in my opinion, usually the preferable form, because of its greater economy of time and expense. It serves the primary purpose just as well as the positive form, which calls for a reply from the customer, for the objective is for the auditor to assure himself that the customer is informed of the amount standing to his debit. If the customer does not admit liability therefor, it is to be assumed he would register an objection just as certainly when the negative form is used as if the positive form were employed. If the customer concurs in the correctness of the amount as stated, no reply is necessary, with consequent economy of postage and of the time otherwise necessary for the handling and checking of the replies.

It is important that in the use of either form of confirmation the procedure be such that undelivered communications to the debtors be returned by the postal authorities directly to the auditor.

Internal Check and Control

The term "internal check and control" has relation to the manner in which the departmentalization and flow of transactions having a financial aspect is arranged in a business concern, and with the apportionment of duties of various members of the concern's staff so that so far as possible the work of recording by one person or department is a check or control on that of others; further, that complete control of the recording of a series of transactions as, for instance, starting from the recording of shipments through to collection of payments made by customers, shall not be in the hands of any one person; and that so far as feasible the handling and recording of funds from customers shall not be by the same person or persons who originate or record the debits to customers or the credits for adjustments in their accounts. Per contra, the incurring and recording of liabilities for materials, merchandise, wages, or expenses shall not be under the control or subject to the unrestricted approval of the person or persons making or recording disbursements. For instance, the recording of the data for and the preparation of the pay roll should not be under the control of those who pay off the men.

The formulation of an opinion, not only of whether a proper system of internal check and control exists, but even more whether it is functioning properly, is difficult at best. The scope of the examination to be made involves two unknown quantities which react upon each other: on the one hand, the nature and extent of the sampling and testing to be made of the recorded transactions must be determined, in part at least, in the light of the system of internal check and control, and, on the other hand, the effectiveness of such a system must be judged to a considerable extent by the results of the auditing tests.

There are differences of opinion among experienced accountants as to the value or otherwise of questionnaires, whether they relate directly to the performance of the work called for by the auditing program or to the features of the system of internal check and control. Some accountants have felt that the use of them has a tendency to emphasize mere routine and to deaden initiative. It may be observed that among doctors the best diagnostician is not necessarily the one who does the best or most complete paper work on a case. Similarly, in the army, the best and most resourceful officer is not necessarily the one most adept in the voluminous paper work which army regulations and practice call for. Nevertheless, in my opinion, it is on the whole desirable that the auditor record the more important features of the system of internal check and control as he makes his inquiry into it for the first time, and that in succeeding audits he note any significant changes that he observes.

It should be understood that when an auditor gives a certificate on the financial statements of a company he is not necessarily endorsing, or completely satisfied with, the system of internal check and control he finds in effect. He has to take it as he finds it for the current examination, and determine how far it shall influence the scope and extent thereof. The number of instances in which the auditor will find an ideal system of internal check and control in existence and functioning 100 per cent to his satisfaction will be relatively few. Human perfection is practically nonexistent. In the final analysis he must determine whether, in all the circumstances and after considering the system as it is in plan, and as it is apparently functioning, he is satisfied that the financial statements do, in his opinion, present fairly the position of the client and the results of its operations for the period under review. Naturally, the effectiveness of the system of internal check will be one of continuing interest to the auditor so that suggestions to the client for the improvement of the system are a logical result of evident defects — or failure to function — which come to the auditor's attention.

Corporate Accounting Control

The McKesson & Robbins case, with its deep-laid conspiracy in high places, gave a tremendous shock to the business and financial world. For some time it was the current topic of conversation in business circles. However, the matter did not remain simply a topic of discussion. The boards of directors of a number of corporations conferred with their independent auditors to acquaint themselves more fully with the scope of the examinations being currently made for their corporations and sought to assure themselves that in its broader aspects "it couldn't happen here."

In the 1938 annual report of one of our largest corporations, which was published soon after the McKesson & Robbins disclosures, the president made a statement concerning the accounting practices and policies of the company, the organization of the accounting functions, the activity of the internal auditing staff, and the examination by the corporation's independent auditors. The purpose of the statement was to describe "how the various items in the financial statements were established in relation to the policies laid down for their determination." In the description of the corporation's accounting organization and methods and the internal check and control the controller played an important part.

A subcommittee of the Stock List Committee of the New York Stock Exchange, in its report of August 11, 1939, made the following recommendation regarding the position and responsibility of the controller:

> More emphasis should be placed on the responsibility of the controller and the assurance to him of adequate authority and facilities. The scope of his responsibilities should be fixed by the board of directors, and he should report periodically to them, in addition to making his customary reports to the operating management.
>
> The controller or chief financial officer should sign the published financial statements of his company, even in those cases where the statements are accompanied by the report of the independent public accountant.
>
> Independent and efficient accounting and internal auditing departments are a vital factor in assuring the accuracy of the books and published reports. The importance of the controller or internal auditor in these connections is paramount and the board of directors should take an active interest in his selection.

Function of the Controller: The Controllers Institute of America has developed the following brief definition of the duties of the controller of a corporation:

> The duties of the controller shall be to maintain adequate records of all assets, liabilities, and transactions of this corporation; to see that adequate audits thereof are currently and regularly made; and, in conjunction with other officers and department heads, to initiate and enforce measures and procedures whereby the business of this corporation shall be conducted with the maximum safety, efficiency, and economy. He shall attend all meetings of the board of directors and of the execu-

tive committee, and he shall report to the president and/or the board of directors as said board of directors may prescribe. His duties and powers shall extend to all subsidiary corporations, and so far as the president may deem practicable, to all affiliated companies.

This definition has been formulated with an eye to the ideal. For instance, the provision that he shall attend all meetings of the board of directors and of the executive committee is at present probably the exception rather than the rule if the controller is not himself a member of the board of directors.

The Controllers Institute has further elaborated on the duties of the controller by enumerating them as follows:

1. The installation and supervision of all accounting records of the corporation.
2. The preparation and interpretation of the financial statements and reports of the corporation.
3. The continuous audit of all accounts and records of the corporation, wherever located.
4. The compilation of production costs.
5. The compilation of costs of distribution.
6. The taking and costing of all physical inventories.
7. The preparation and filing of tax returns and the supervision of all matters relating to taxes.
8. The preparation and interpretation of all statistical records and reports of the corporation.
9. The preparation, as budget director, in conjunction with other officers and department heads, of an annual budget covering all activities of the corporation, for submission to the board of directors prior to the beginning of the fiscal year. The authority of the controller, with respect to the veto of commitments or expenditures not authorized by the budget, shall, from time to time, be fixed by the board of directors.
10. The ascertainment currently that the properties of the corporation are properly and adequately insured.
11. The initiation, preparation, and issuance of standard practices relating to all accounting matters and procedures and the coordination of systems throughout the corporation, including clerical and office methods, records, reports and procedures.
12. The maintenance of adequate records of authorized appropria-

tions and the determination that all sums expended pursuant thereto are properly accounted for.

13. The ascertainment currently that financial transactions covered by minutes of the board of directors and/or the Executive Committee are properly executed and recorded.

14. The maintenance of adequate records of all contracts and leases.

15. The approval for payment (and/or countersigning) of all checks, promissory notes, and other negotiable instruments of the corporation which have been signed by the treasurer or such other officers as shall have been authorized by the by-laws of the corporation or from time to time designated by the board of directors.

16. The examination of all warrants for the withdrawal of securities from the vaults of the corporation and the determination that such withdrawals are made in conformity with the by-laws and/or regulations established from time to time by the board of directors.

17. The preparation or approval of the regulations or standard practices required to assure compliance with orders or regulations issued by duly constituted governmental agencies.

Internal Auditing: An important contribution toward an effective system of internal check and control, especially for large companies, is the use of an internal auditing staff. Its work is to conduct a continuous audit which will be more extensive as to detailed examination or verification of the various classes of transactions recorded in the corporation's accounts than is practicable for the independent auditor. In the present day the extent and complexity of the business of a large, and often far-flung, corporation requires the independent auditor to devote a large part of his time to the study of the accounting principles applied by the corporation and the consistency with which they have been followed from period to period.

The more that internal auditing is utilized as a safeguard against peculations and in order to insure proper accounting for the avails of the business done, the more the independent auditor can devote his attention to the consideration of the proper application of sound accounting principles and the formulation of his opinion regarding the dependability of the financial statements which the management submits to stockholders and creditors.

Among the salient features of the organization and work of an internal auditing staff or department and of its relation to the work of the independent auditor may be mentioned the following:

Distinction between work of the internal auditor and that of the independent auditor: One consideration in establishing an internal auditing organization is that the cost of auditing may be lessened by reason of the independent auditor's being justified in relying on the detailed examination and verification by the internal auditor. Especially in this day of the widespread use of mechanical bookkeeping appliances, it would involve unwarranted expense to have the independent auditor devote himself to the detailed checking of the bookkeeping records. By confining the auditing work of the independent auditor to test checks of the accounts and to reviewing the reports of the internal auditors, he can devote his efforts primarily to those matters which are of major importance in reviewing the financial statements of position and operations and the manner in which the various items appearing therein have been built up.

In distinguishing between the work of the internal auditor and that of the independent auditor, it may be noted that the former is likely to be engaged in verifying transactions in the light of accounting policies laid down by the management, whereas it is the function of the latter to determine whether or not those accounting policies are sound.

Coordination of work of the internal auditor with that of the independent auditor: Programs of coordination must be individually developed according to the particular needs and form of organization of different companies. A few general points may be mentioned for consideration when such a program of coordination is being formulated:

(a) From the very nature of his work, the internal auditor will have a familiarity with the everyday routine and details of the business of which the independent auditor should avail himself, both by reviewing such formal reports as the internal auditor may make to his superiors and by conference on those matters arising in the course of the independent examination concerning which the internal auditor should be able to give information;

(b) In determining the scope and extent of the independent auditor's examination, the field covered by the internal auditor and the apparent effectiveness — or otherwise — of his work should be considered by the former;

(c) When a corporation has many branches and a number of factories spread over a wide geographical area, the independent auditor will not necessarily visit all of them every year. In such cases the work of the internal auditor will supplement that of the independent auditor in respect of the points not visited in a particular year;

(d) In some instances the internal auditor may, under the direction of the independent auditor, prepare analyses, schedules, and accounting exhibits which the latter may require. This procedure may be considered as supplementary to the normal practice of having the accounting department prepare various schedules for use in the audit.

Significant types of auditing work by the internal auditor: The work of the internal auditor is closely related in many respects to the work of the independent auditor, but in most cases he will go further in making detailed verifications. There is not always the necessity to verify completely all the transactions, however, for in many cases a "spot test" would be quite sufficient. The exercise of judgment on the part of the internal auditor, therefore, is without question a basic factor in the efficient conduct of his activities.

(a) Participation by the internal auditor in inventory taking has in many corporations become one of his important duties. The internal auditor is regarded as being in a favorable position to accept this responsibility because of his familiarity with the company's product and the absence of the limitations of time which are necessarily placed on the independent auditor. The internal auditor can actively participate in the taking of the inventory and is aided by his continuing familiarity with the unit quantities and values of his company's materials and products.

(b) In large companies, the purchasing process is usually classified into various steps, and most of the normal purchasing progresses along such routine steps. It is not difficult for the internal auditor to verify the generality of the purchases and the classification of them; however, he may have a few special problems with which to contend. Certain commodities may be of a perishable nature and must be purchased as needed; also some departments or personnel find it necessary to make special purchases, as, for example, repair parts. It is instances such as these that sometimes require the internal auditor to go into considerable detail to see that these items are properly handled for accounting purposes. Purchases are sometimes made for direct shipment to customers, and the internal auditor should follow these transactions through to see that the customers were properly charged. Purchase returns are another class of item to be looked into carefully and in detail by the internal auditor.

(c) The accounting aspects of the sales procedures which are the concern of the internal auditor center about the satisfactory establishment of accountability, entailing adequate inventory control, shipping or delivery procedures, and, in the case of cash sales and scrap sales, suitable control over such transactions. He is also concerned about the provision of adequate managerial information for control, which requires adequate analysis of sales transactions and current reports covering these data for management use. The duties assigned to the internal auditor may also include inquiry into the service aspects of the sales transactions, the promptness of delivery, accuracy of filling the orders, systematically and accurately prepared billing papers, and general courteous treatment in all matters in respect to customer relations.

Work of the internal auditor not strictly limited to the realm of accounting: The close relationship of the internal auditor to the management provides the latter with a means for gaining special information needed for dealing effectively with particular problems. For instance, it may be necessary to establish further the accuracy of certain company information and to analyze its bearing upon a proposed contract. In such a case the internal auditor may be required to go into facts surrounding the proposed transaction beyond their strict accounting significance and report upon practices or policies which are involved. Again, he may have the task of examining and appraising the reasonableness of the bases on which intercompany or interdepartmental relations rest and the general accuracy with which charges and credits between them are made. The extreme importance of budgetary activities as a means of effective management control may make it necessary to use the internal auditor for review and appraisal of such activities, either completely or in respect of particular aspects thereof.

These are only a few illustrations of special duties of the internal auditor. The internal auditing staff may be considered to be a flexible group which, in addition to regular duties, is ready to function in whatever manner will most effectively serve the management of a corporation.

Organization of internal auditing staff or department: In order that such a department serve effectively, it should have a status in the organization independent of other departments which must come under its review and appraisal. It is desirable that the head of the department be responsible directly to the controller or to another officer who is above the direct functional activities, the accounting of which is being audited. The size of the internal auditing staff will necessarily vary with the needs of the corporation. Although the staff members may be classified, either by rank (such as executive, senior, semisenior, or junior) or by operating divisions (such as factory, retail, warehouse, or traveling), it is desirable not to continue staff members in the same routine or geographical area over too extended a period of time. Rotation of assignment with a fresh mind coming to a particular field or section of the accounts, though under the continued direction of the head of the department, has its values.

The headquarters of the internal auditing department will normally be at the head office of the corporation. In addition to the chief auditor, those staff members concerned chiefly with the auditing activity at the central office will be stationed there. The size and character of personnel, the nature and scope of the internal auditing program, and the management policies in respect thereof will naturally have to be worked out in the light of any limitations imposed by the funds made available for the department.

The auditing program should include provision for reports to be made by staff members, not only at completion of a particular assignment, but also during the progress thereof if special circumstances develop during an assignment. Concurrent study of the corporation's accounting practices should be part of the work of the internal auditor with recommendations for any simplification and improved control as the natural result.

Conservatism in Financial Statements

As the auditor proceeds with his work he is likely to get an impression whether the accounting policy of the management is conservative or otherwise. The provision made for uncollectible receivables; the manner in which the inventory is priced, and especially the treatment of goods which have been on hand for a considerable length of time and in which styles may have changed or which are shopworn; the provisions for depreciation and depletion; the resolving of the doubt in favor of charging borderline items to operations rather than capitalizing them or, conversely, the attempt to nurse earnings by capitalizing everything that can possibly be claimed as an addition to or improvement of plant; the liberality of and promptness of provision for possible losses, or for claims of one kind or another against the concern or an evident policy of deferring write-offs as long as possible, all contribute to the feeling which the experienced auditor gains either that the accounting policy of his client is conservative or the reverse. Sometimes the auditor will find that ultraconservatism has reigned and that it has led to understatement of earnings or possibly to equalization thereof between years by taking advantage in less favorable years of the ultraconservatism of other years. Inventories, perhaps, have been priced at below either cost or market and, if no disclosure of the practice has been made, a secret reserve has thus been created.

It seems likely that, taken by and large, any substantial secret reserves which had been built up in the accounts of corporate enterprise generally in the United States would probably have been exhausted by the losses of the depression period. In fact, it seems likely that this was generally true as early in the depression period as 1933. To the Americans present at the International Congress of Accounting held in London in July of that year, however, it was interesting to note the animated discussion by the British accountants which followed extended reference to secret reserves in the paper presented by Mr. Henry Morgan, F.S.A.A., past president of the Society of Incorporated Accountants and Auditors, on "The Auditor's Responsibility in Relation to Balance Sheets and Profit and Loss Accounts" from the British point of view.

I had the privilege of hearing the discussion and judged

from the interest in the subject that secret reserves are (or at least were) more often present in the case of British corporations than is the case on this side of the ocean. One of the British accountants told me it was supposed that the large London banks had heavy secret reserves because when some heavy loss was incurred — as, for instance, due to the notorious Hatry failure — the banks were able to absorb it without any apparent effect on their surplus and undivided profits.

It is not always easy to keep on an absolutely even keel in making accounting decisions or distinctions in classifying expenditures as falling into either the capital or the expense class. In deciding what should be the amount of provision for possible losses or matters in litigation, in determining the allowances to be made for depreciation and depletion, the ultimate outcome of which cannot be known for years to come, etc., judgment is bound to lean to one side or the other, and I am frank to say that I am in favor of an accounting policy that leans toward the conservative side. Conservatism, however, must not go so far as to distort the presentation of the financial position and the operating results.

This is particularly a case in which disclosure is of the essence. I do not believe that present-day accounting practice in the United States justifies an ultraconservative accounting policy which would give rise to secret reserves (directly or indirectly) without disclosure, though I recognize the difficulty of laying down any definition of, or determining when, a "reasonable" point has been passed. Obviously, each case must be determined on its own facts. However, I am here setting forth the substance of a tentative statement of general principles to be followed when dealing with secret reserves, which I formulated while I was listening to the above-mentioned discussion of the subject in London in 1933:

(1) If the reserves are not required to provide for any contingent liabilities or to provide for any uncertainties of value in respect of any assets, such reserves are in effect a portion of the company's surplus and, if of relatively material amount, there is no accounting principle which justifies the failure to disclose the amount and nature of such reserves in the balance sheet; further, any reserves of such character should at the time of creation be treated as an allocation of profits or surplus and not be merged or obscured in the profit and loss (or income) statement;

(2) If the so-called "reserves" represent a provision for the amount which it is believed may be required for the discharge of liabilities which are only momentarily contingent, or which represent a reasonable exercise of conservatism in valuing assets, disclosure of the specific amounts of such reserves in either balance sheet or profit and loss statement does not seem essential; also, in such a case the items come nearer to being provisions or allowances than reserves;

(3) When reserves of the character contemplated in (1) are discontinued, the amount thereof should be credited directly to surplus and not passed through the profit and loss statement of the year of such discontinuance;

(4) In the event of any charges being made to reserves of the character contemplated in (1), the nature and amount of such charge should be disclosed in the year in which made, in most cases preferably in the year's profit and loss statement;

(5) In the event of its being found that any material portion of reserves contemplated in (2) is no longer required, such amount should be credited to surplus account (to earned surplus, if the debit was to earned surplus) or, if included in the year's profit and loss statement, the amount should be described as an extraordinary item (not merely merged in the ordinary operations) and added to the net result from current operations for the year.

III. THE AUDITOR'S REPORT

THE EXAMINATION of the statements of a business or financial enterprise is, in the final analysis, but a stepping-stone to the preparation of a report by the independent auditor on the financial statements which are the subject of his review. In the case of large corporations with well-organized accounting departments the statements may be prepared by the client's staff and come to the auditor with the approval of the principal financial officer in practically the form in which it is expected they will be published to the stockholders or other interested parties, or be filed with the Securities and Exchange Commission or other regulatory bodies, or otherwise utilized. In the case of some concerns the statements may, in fact, be prepared by the auditor from the books after giving effect to the results of his examination, in which event he will naturally discuss with the client any adjustments which may have been made in the figures as shown on the face of the books, and the form of presentation to be used. As to any such adjustments, the auditor will naturally seek to obtain the concurrence of the client. In either event, the statements are regarded as the representations of the client. In the former event they are not only theoretically so but even physically so. In the latter event they are so because the client adopts them as his and decides whether they shall be promulgated.

In both instances the disclosure of all material facts essential to a proper understanding of the position of the enterprise and of the results of operations for the indicated period is most important. The standard of disclosure which should ever be before the auditor in considering his responsibilities when reporting on the statements is well stated in the requirement of the Securities Act of 1933 that as to "any part of the registration statement purporting to be made upon his authority as an expert or purporting to be a copy of or extract from a report . . . of himself as an expert, he had after reasonable investigation, reasonable ground to believe and did believe, at the time such part of the registration statement became effective, that the statements therein were true and that there was no omission to state a material fact required to be stated therein or necessary to make the statements therein not misleading. . . ."

There might seem to be cases where the question of disclosing data which is not obvious or implicit in the items of the financial statements themselves is rather academic because of the statements relating to the affairs of a close corporation or a partnership or proprietorship and all those who are likely to see the statements are already fully informed as to the affairs of the concern. Detailed disclosure might in such instances seem almost superfluous. Yet even in such instances the auditor must, if he makes no reservation or qualification in his report, require disclosure in the spirit of the requirement above quoted from the Securities Act because he can never know what use may be made of his report or into whose hands it may come.

Reliance on the apparent absence of privity of contract between the auditor and third parties into whose hands the report may come would be ill-advised. Especially where there are those who have an interest in the affairs of a closely held concern other than the direct management, as, for example, bank and merchandise creditors, it is of the utmost importance that all essential disclosures be made. Such disclosures may relate to many different circumstances as, for example, hypothecation of certain assets, commitments other than those in the ordinary course of business, contingent liabilities, restrictions on surplus arising out of bond indentures or holdings of treasury stock, most or all of which would not ordinarily appear on the face of the client's books of account.

Explanatory notes on, or appended to, financial statements are not in themselves a recent development. To some extent they have been used ever since the inclusion of certified financial statements in prospectuses or security offerings became at all general. However, the use, both in number and in scope, of notes appended to the balance sheet and the income statement received a stimulus from the passage of the Securities Act. The auditor, in taking seriously his responsibilities when certifying the financial statements to be included in registration statements, whether for new security issues or as annual reports required to be filed with the Securities and Exchange Commission, felt it essential that there be adequate disclosure of material information which would not normally or readily appear on the face of the formal financial statements but which is essential to an understanding of the position and operating results of the reporting company.

Directors and officers, also, and especially their counsel, have in most instances favored fullest disclosure of pertinent information in statements coming within the scope of the Securities Acts, so that there might be no question later as to anyone having been misled by lack of adequate disclosure of material facts and circumstances. Indeed, the question has been raised whether the precautions taken to make sure that no desirable disclosure has been omitted have not, in some instances at least, led to such a flood of explanatory notes that the financial statements proper are overshadowed by the volume of explanatory matter which must be studied at great length before the reader may draw dependable conclusions from the balance sheet and the income statement.

To some extent this is an illustration of the human tendency to go from one extreme to the other. Forty or fifty years ago reports to stockholders and bankers' prospectuses almost invariably contained extremely condensed financial statements, and the reader had to rely on his imagination to a considerable extent as to various phases of the company's financial position or its operations. A majority of the industrial corporations publishing reports at that time did not disclose the amount of their sales, and very often the income statement contained only a few items beginning with the operating profit after the manufacturing costs and selling and administrative expenses had been deducted from the sales.

The disclosure of essential information which can be made in the description of items on the face of the financial statements has undergone improvement, and in the ordinary case the nature or volume of it is not such as to raise any question as to the need for it. It is in respect of the notes appended to the balance sheet and income statement that the volume in some instances is such as to raise the question whether it may not defeat the purpose of the notes. In the words of the old adage, the woods cannot be seen for the trees.

Although the heavy responsibilities of the Securities Acts, and the tendency of the courts to bear down on the accountant and directors in respect of their legal liabilities to a degree which seems at times unreasonable, have naturally led to extreme caution to insure full disclosure of all material information, nevertheless a balanced viewpoint should prevail. In the first place, notes regarding nonessential or relatively immaterial matters should not be unduly elaborated; in fact, they should when feasible be excluded. Further, and this is still more important, explanatory notes should not be resorted to as an "out" in respect of items which ought to be adjusted. An item in either the balance sheet or income account which is in itself not properly stated cannot be satisfactorily dealt with by a note indicating that it has some other significance or should otherwise be interpreted than one would infer from a reading of the statements. In other words, as Mr. J. M. B. Hoxsey, who for so many years rendered such valuable service to the New York Stock Exchange, sometimes said, "A note reading that, assuming that two and two make five, such and such would be the result, is not a warranted substitute for correct treatment of an item in the financial statements."

As to reasonable disclosure of financial information to its stockholders, the annual reports of the United States Steel Corporation, practically from its organization some forty years ago, were regarded by accountants and other students of financial affairs as heralding the beginning of a better day. For a long time relatively few industrial corporations emulated its example. After the First World War, however, and particularly during the past decade, there was marked improvement, and it may be said that today there are a substantial number of corporations which put out reports containing financial statements that meet the requirements of: (a) sufficiently detailed presentation of both position and operations to give the stockholder an intelligent understanding of the results of the company's activities and of its present position, (b) satisfactory form of presentation, and (c) supplemental explanatory information required for the understanding of items in the financial statements which have special features, or for the presentation of matters which are still indeterminate or otherwise are not susceptible of definite inclusion in the formal statements.

I do not wish to imply that we have reached the ideal in respect of published corporate reports. Many companies have not yet attained the standard set by those who have led with a good example. I do wish to emphasize, however, that over the years there has been marked progress and that the improvement was already evident before the incidence of those influences which, during the past decade, have contributed substantially to improvement in both form and substance of published financial statements.

Evolution of the Auditor's "Certificate"

In the course of time auditors' reports have become broadly classified as being of either the long form or the short form of report, the latter being also colloquially referred to as a "certificate." The long form of report is not standardized and should not be, for it is to be used in those instances in which there are reasons for bringing to the client's attention varied information and details concerning the financial statements which have been under examination, such as particular features of the scope of the examination, significant developments calling for extended descriptive text, comments on the accounting methods in use, possible criticisms, suggestions respecting the treatment of various items or the improvement of the client's accounting methods, and so on. The report of this type should be anything but stereotyped. It relates to a particular engagement, with the circumstances peculiar to it, and should be framed accordingly. Obviously, it should be so organized and expressed that it will be informing and intelligible to the client and of real assistance to him.

A word or two of caution regarding the use of the long form of report may not be amiss. If the examination is limited in any way, or if the results are such that the auditor has any reservations or believes qualifications to be in order, the report should bring out the facts clearly. He should not rely on stating in his report merely the work done and leaving to inference the omission of other work which would be required for an unrestricted examination.

The short form of report or certificate grew out of the need for setting forth briefly the opinion of the auditor upon the financial statements submitted to stockholders, bond holders, banks, or others to whom the client wishes to submit primarily the financial statements. It was felt that the primary purpose of the auditor's report in such circumstances is to indicate that an examination had been made by an independent accountant, and that in his opinion the balance sheet and related statements of income and surplus set forth fairly the position of the corporation, partnership, or individual enterprise, and the results of its operations for a given period.

In the course of time a brief form developed which with minor modifications was widely used, and which read in substance as follows:

> We have examined the accounts of the Blank Company as at ...., 19......, and
>
> We certify that, in our opinion, the above balance sheet correctly sets forth the company's financial position on that date and the accompanying income account correctly summarizes the results of its operations for the year then ended.

When only a balance sheet was being published or otherwise utilized, the clause relating to the income account was omitted from the certificate.

In 1932 the Special Committee of the American Institute of Accountants on Cooperation with Stock Exchanges began a careful consideration of the general line of development of the activities of the New York Stock Exchange in relation to the annual reports of corporations. The work of the Institute Committee led to its recommendation of a form of auditor's report reading as follows:

> To the XYZ Company:
>
> We have made an examination of the balance sheet of the XYZ Company as at December 31, 1933, and of the statement of income and surplus for the year 1933. In connection therewith, we examined or tested accounting records of the Company and other supporting evidence and obtained information and explanations from officers and employees of the Company; we also made a general review of the accounting methods and of the operating and income accounts for the year, but we did not make a detailed audit of the transactions.
>
> In our opinion, based upon such examination, the accompanying balance-sheet and related statement of income and surplus fairly present, in accordance with accepted principles of accounting consistently maintained by the Company during the year under review, its position at December 31, 1933, and the results of its operations for the year.

The publication of this form of report or certificate by the Institute included the following notes regarding its use:

Notes

1. It is contemplated that before signing a report of the type suggested, the accountant should have at least made an examination of the character outlined in the bulletin, "Verification of Financial Statements," as interpreted in the communication of the Committee on Stock List to the Governing Committee dated October 24, 1933.

2. The report should be addressed to the directors of the company or to the stockholders, if the appointment is made by them.

3. The statement of what has been examined would, of course, conform to the titles of the accounts or statements reported upon.

4. In the second sentence, any special forms of confirmation could be mentioned: e.g., "including confirmation of cash and securities by inspection or certificates from depositaries."

5. This certificate is appropriate only if the accounting for the year is consistent in basis with that for the preceding year. If there has been any material change either in accounting principles or in the manner of their application, the nature of the change should be indicated.

6. It is contemplated that the form of report would be modified when and as necessary to embody any qualifications, reservations or supplementary explanations.

This report was so framed as to constitute answers to the following questions:

1. Whether, in the auditor's opinion, the form of the balance sheet and of the income, or profit and loss account, is such as fairly to present the financial position and the results of operation;

2. Whether the accounts, in the auditor's opinion, are fairly determined on the basis of consistent application of the system of accounting regularly employed by the company;

3. Whether, in the auditor's opinion, such system of accounting conforms to accepted accounting practices.

It was felt that the auditor's report or certificate should make it clear that a detailed audit had not been made, even though it might well be assumed that the business and investing public would so understand. Consequently, there was inserted in the suggested form of report, after the description in general terms of the scope of the examination, the clause "but we did not make a detailed audit of the transactions."

It is interesting to note that the Chairman of the Committee of the Controllers' Institute of America on Stock Exchange Relations, with which committee the Exchange also conferred, expressed himself warmly in favor of a standard form of certificate, one paragraph in the committee's communication to the Exchange reading as follows:

> We recognize the fact that agreement on terminology is always very difficult, because most people have certain preferences of language, and for this reason, we can see that agreement by public accountants on a particular form may not be easy to secure. We urge, however, that the Stock Exchange stress the necessity for such uniformity of language as to the major body of the certificate with the committee of the American Institute of Accountants, so that as far as possible all accounting firms will use the same language for the main part of their certificate. The wording of specific exceptions and qualifications, we appreciate, would naturally have to be left to the individual firms, since standardization to that extent we do not believe to be practicable.

The suggested standard short form of report (certificate) met with almost instant and widespread acceptance. Although the final communication containing the suggested form and the correspondence which preceded its adoption [1] were not published until January 21, 1934, the suggested form was used for the great majority of reports published by listed companies for the calendar year 1933.

This form of report continued in general use until 1939. At that time a special committee of the American Institute of Accountants, appointed after the McKesson & Robbins development, recommended the following "Short Form of Independent Certified Public Accountant's Report or Opinion":

[1] Published in pamphlet form by the American Institute of Accountants under the title of *Audits of Corporate Accounts.*

To the Board of Directors (or Stockholders) of the XYZ Company:

We have examined the balance-sheet of the XYZ Company as of April 30, 1939, and the statements of income and surplus for the fiscal year then ended, have reviewed the system of internal control and the accounting procedures of the company and, without making a detailed audit of the transactions, have examined or tested accounting records of the company and other supporting evidence by methods and to the extent we deemed appropriate.

In our opinion, the accompanying balance-sheet and related statements of income and surplus present fairly the position of the XYZ Company at April 30, 1939, and the results of its operations for the fiscal year, in conformity with generally accepted accounting principles applied on a basis consistent with that of the preceding year.

The Committee emphasized that "while the proposed form is submitted as a standard, it is not prescribed or recommended for invariable use but should be adapted to the needs of the particular case."

Aside from some minor improvements in phraseology, the revised form in my judgment does not represent any marked improvement of the form promulgated in 1934, or convey any greater understanding to the lay reader concerning the nature of the examination or of the opinion expressed by the accountant on the financial statements. The first paragraph of the 1939 form, in slightly different language, has the same content as the corresponding paragraph of the 1934 form: (a) it identifies the financial statements which have been the subject of the examination; (b) it describes the general character of the examination, viz., by audit tests and a review of the accounting methods; and (c) it emphasizes that a detailed audit was not made. In addition, the 1939 revision stressed the obvious, viz., that the examination was by methods and to the extent which accorded with the judgment of the accountant.

It was first proposed to eliminate from the revised form the explicit statement that the examination did not include a detailed audit of the transactions, the committee's thought being that a sufficient period had elapsed since the adoption of the 1934 form to make further use of this emphasis unnecessary. It is interesting that some expressions of opinion, not only from within but also from without the profession, indicated a feeling that a longer period of education of the business and investing public was desirable, and the substance of the phrase was therefore continued in the revised form.

The second paragraph of the 1939 revision embodied two changes from the 1934 form: One was the elimination of the phrase "based upon such examination" which was inserted in the original form to link explicitly the opinion with the examination described in the previous paragraph; the other was the explicit relation of consistency of the latest statements (as to the application of generally accepted accounting principles) to the corresponding statements of the preceding year. The latter was deemed desirable in the interest of precision; it seemed better than reliance upon the note which had been promulgated as one of six explanatory notes with the 1934 form of the report. That note reads as follows:

> This certificate is appropriate only if the accounting for the year is consistent in basis with that for the preceding year. If there has been any material change either in accounting principles or in the manner of their application, the nature of the change should be indicated.

When the Federal Trade Commission, which was originally charged with the administration of the Securities Act, promulgated its first rules and regulations relating to that act, it included therein the following article in respect of the auditor's certificate:

> Any certificate by an independent certified or public accountant with respect to any part of the registration statement, any papers or documents used in connection therewith, shall be dated and shall state that such accountant . . . has, after reasonable investigation, reasonable grounds to believe, and does believe, at the time of the date of such

certificate, that the statements therein are true and that there is no omission to state a material fact required to be stated therein or necessary to make the statements therein not misleading, except as specifically noted.

If in any case such accountant . . . is unable to satisfy himself concerning the correctness of any item in the said part of the registration statement, papers or documents, he shall refer to such items in his certificate and give appropriate explanation thereof.

If anything comes to the attention of such accountant . . . or he obtains knowledge of any facts before the effective date of registration which would make any of the material items therein untrue or indicate that there was an omission to state a material fact required to be stated or necessary to make the statements therein not misleading, he shall bring such immediately to the attention of the Commission.

In determining what constitutes reasonable investigation and reasonable grounds for belief, the standard of reasonableness shall be that required of a person occupying a fiduciary relationship.

Where a partnership of certified or public accountants certifies to a registration statement or any part thereof or any document used in connection therewith, the certificate shall be signed with the partnership name and by a member thereof.

Some months later the Commission amended the first paragraph of the article quoted above to read as follows:

Any certificate by an independent certified or public accountant with respect to a registration statement or any papers or documents used in connection therewith shall be dated and shall conclude with a statement substantially to the following effect:

> "Subject to the foregoing comments, we have, after reasonable investigation, reasonable grounds to believe, and do believe, at the date of this certificate, that the statements contained in the attached balance sheets and in the attached profit and loss statements truly and fairly reflect the application of accepted accounting practice to the facts disclosed by our investigation, and that there is no omission to state a material fact required to be stated therein or necessary to make the statements therein not misleading."

It will be noted that the Federal Trade Commission sought to have the auditor's certificate include language similar to that used in Article 11 of the Securities Act, to which I have already referred as establishing broadly the standard of disclosure to be followed in the preparation of financial statements.

Upon the passage of the Securities Exchange Act in 1934, the Securities and Exchange Commission succeeded the Federal Trade Commission as administrator of the Securities Act of 1933, as well as of the Securities Exchange Act.

The onerous nature of the liability provisions of the 1933 Act was charged by financiers and businessmen with being responsible for impeding public financing. The new Securities and Exchange Commission under the vigorous leadership of its chairman had a study made of the situation and revised the forms, instructions, and general rules and regulations for the administration of the Securities Act. In addition it prepared those applicable to the newly enacted Securities Exchange Act. In this study and in the formulation of recommendations to the Commission, which it adopted for the purpose of breaking the "log jam" affecting financing, a member of the faculty of the Harvard Graduate School of Business Administration, Dr. T. H. Sanders, rendered important service.

The Securities and Exchange Commission abandoned the rule of the Federal Trade Commission which, as already indicated, prescribed at least a portion of the language to be used in the auditor's certificate when appended to financial statements filed with the Commission, and promulgated the following rule:

> The certificate of the accountant or accountants shall be dated, shall be reasonably comprehensive as to the scope of the audit made, and shall state clearly the opinion of the accountant or accountants in respect of the financial statements of, and the accounting principles and procedures followed by, the person or persons whose statements are furnished. In certifying to the financial statements, independent public or independent certified public accountants may give due weight to an internal system of audit regularly maintained by means of auditors employed on the registrant's own staff. In such case the independent accountants shall review the accounting procedures followed by the

registrant and its subsidiaries and by appropriate measures shall satisfy themselves that such accounting procedures are in fact being followed. Nothing in this rule shall be construed to imply authority for the omission of any procedure which independent public accountants would ordinarily employ in the course of a regular annual audit. The certificate of the accountant or accountants shall be applicable to the matter in the registration statement proper to which a reference is required in the financial statements.

Following the adoption of this rule, the Commission accepted registration statements in which the financial statements bore the certificate of accountants in the customary Institute form, amplified by either explanations or qualifications, when called for by the circumstances of a particular case.

In the report of the Securities and Exchange Commission on its investigation in the matter of McKesson & Robbins, Inc., the Commission expressed its views concerning the principles on which it believed the form and content of the auditor's certificate should be based. Subsequently, it revised its rule (effective March 1, 1941) regarding the contents of accountants' certificates appended to financial statements filed with the Commission pursuant to the several securities acts and similar legislation, so as to read as follows:

(a) *Technical requirements*

The accountant's certificate shall be dated, shall be signed manually, and shall identify without detailed enumeration the financial statements covered by the certificate.

(b) *Representations as to the audit*

The accountant's certificate (i) shall contain a reasonably comprehensive statement as to the scope of the audit made including, if with respect to significant items in the financial statements any auditing procedures generally recognized as normal have been omitted, a specific designation of such procedures and of the reasons for their omission; (ii) shall state whether the audit was made in accordance with generally accepted auditing standards applicable in the circumstances; and (iii) shall state whether the audit made omitted any procedure deemed necessary by the accountant under the circumstances of the particular case.

In determining the scope of the audit necessary, appropriate consideration shall be given to the adequacy of the system of internal check and control. Due weight may be given to an internal system of audit regularly maintained by means of auditors employed on the registrant's own staff. The accountant shall review the accounting procedures followed by the person or persons whose statements are certified and by appropriate measures shall satisfy himself that such accounting procedures are in fact being followed.

Nothing in this rule shall be construed to imply authority for the omission of any procedure which independent accountants would ordinarily employ in the course of an audit made for the purpose of expressing the opinions required by paragraph (c) of this rule.

(c) *Opinions to be expressed*

The accountant's certificate shall state clearly:

(i) the opinion of the accountant in respect of the financial statements covered by the certificate and the accounting principles and practices reflected therein;

(ii) the opinion of the accountant as to any change in accounting principles or practices, or adjustments of the accounts, required to be set forth by rule 3-07; and

(iii) the nature of, and the opinion of the accountant as to, any significant differences between the accounting principles and practices reflected in the financial statements and those reflected in the accounts after the entry of adjustments for the period under review.

(d) *Exceptions*

Any matters to which the accountant takes exception shall be clearly identified, the exception thereto specifically and clearly stated, and, to the extent practicable, the effect of each such exception on the related financial statements given.

One material change in the rule, it will be noted, was the requirement that, "if with respect to significant items in the financial statements any auditing procedures generally recognized as normal have been omitted, a specific designation of such procedures and of the reasons for their omission" shall be included in the auditor's statement of the scope of his examination. A similar requirement had been recommended in the original report of the special committee of the American Institute of Accountants on auditing procedure which had been appointed immediately after the disclosure of the McKesson & Robbins conspiracy. Upon further consideration, however, the committee came to the conclusion that such a requirement would not be desirable and stated in its later report that it is the responsibility of the accountant — and one which he cannot escape — to determine the scope of the examination which he should make before giving his opinion on the statements under review. If in his judgment it is not practicable and reasonable in the circumstances of a given engagement to undertake the auditing procedures regarding inventories and/or receivables set forth in this report as generally accepted procedure, and he has satisfied himself by other methods regarding such inventories and/or receivables, no useful purpose will be served by requiring an explanation in his report. If physical tests of inventories and/or confirmation of receivables are practicable and reasonable and the auditor has omitted such generally accepted auditing procedure, he should make a clear-cut exception in his report.

Unfortunately the Commission did not seem to grasp the underlying philosophy of the Institute committee's mature conclusion, namely, that to state in the auditor's certificate that a given procedure had not been considered practicable and reasonable, even though satisfactory reasons for the omission be given, merely tends to confuse the reader of the certificate. The average reader would certainly not be able to determine from such a statement whether the omission was justified. Even another accountant would hesitate to say whether, despite the explanation given, the omission was justified without some examination on his part into the circumstances of the particular case. All of which leads up to the query of what useful purpose is served by seeking, in effect, to have the reader of the certificate attempt to form an opinion as to the adequacy or otherwise of the scope of the examination. No amount of regulation can supply lack of competency or integrity in performing professional service. Loss of professional standing — the severest form of loss to the practitioner — is the penalty for the former, and the liabilities of the law are the penalty for the latter.

Another material change in the Commission's rule was the addition of the requirement that in his certificate the auditor "shall state whether the audit was made in accordance with accepted auditing standards applicable in the circumstances." In the Commission's release accompanying its promulgation of the revised rule regarding accountants' certificates, it was explained that "in referring to generally accepted auditing standards the Commission has in mind, in addition to the employment of generally recognized normal auditing procedures, their application with professional competence by properly trained persons."

It seems strange that the Commission, the membership of which includes men with a professional background, such as lawyers, should have considered it necessary to require the accountant to emphasize his professional competence. It would seem rather odd if a lawyer in writing his opinion on a real estate title were to include therein a solemn statement to the effect that he was competent to examine real estate titles or that he had conducted his examination in a professionally competent manner. I cannot imagine an engineer who is making a report on his examination into the soundness of a bridge or other engineering project including therein a paragraph emphasizing his competence as an engineer and the performance of his engagement in accordance with accepted engineering standards. Surely, a doctor or surgeon called in as a consultant to express an opinion on the diagnosis of a difficult case of illness would not feel that in making a written report thereon he need include any statement of his professional competence or that he had made his examination of the patient in accordance with accepted medical or surgical standards applicable in the circumstances.

A physician was recently sued in New Jersey for damages by the parents of a child who contended that he had not handled the case properly. One of the experts for the defense, a man of eminent reputation in the particular field of medicine in which the case arose, testified, as stated in a newspaper report of the trial, that "Doctor ——— (the defendant) had in his (the witness's) opinion exercised the degree of knowledge, skill, and care usual in the general practice of medicine." The quoted sentence seems to me to state in a minimum of words the implied representation that any practitioner, not merely in medicine but in any profession, whether law, engineering, or accounting, makes when he undertakes to serve a client professionally, namely, professional competence and such performance as may be reasonably expected in the circumstances of the case. A specific statement thereof in the accountant's certificate seems superfluous and merely results in burdening the certificate with unnecessary phraseology.

In the endeavor, however, to cooperate as fully as possible with the Commission, the American Institute of Accountants waived the objections which it saw to the aforementioned requirements of the Commission's revised rule, and proposed the addition of the following sentence to the first paragraph of the 1939 form of Institute certificate:

> In our opinion, our examination was made in accordance with generally accepted auditing standards applicable in the circumstances and included all procedures which we considered necessary.

In further discussions between representatives of the Institute and of the Commission, the former emphasized the fact that the proposed addition to the Institute form of certificate must be based on opinion. The Commission, without questioning that fact, indicated that it regarded the new sentence as "a positive representation consistent with the implied representation he (the auditor) makes by holding himself out as a professional and expert accountant or auditor," and said that the proposed use of the words "in our opinion" appeared to be inconsistent with Section (b) (ii) of the revised rule.

In order to avoid an impasse with the Commission and upon being advised by counsel that, regardless of whether the statement was made categorically (without the use of the words, "in our opinion"), or specifically as a matter of opinion, it could be in fact only a statement of opinion, the Institute decided not to pursue the matter further. Consequently, accountants omit the words "in our opinion" from the aforementioned new sentence added to the 1939 Institute form of certificate, in respect of financial statements filed with the Commission since the effective date of the revised rule.

The question has naturally been considered by practicing accountants whether this addition to the Institute form of certificate should be confined to those cases in which the financial statements are filed with the Securities and Exchange Commission or whether it should be used generally whenever the short form of report (certificate) is appropriate. Unless the Commission feels led in the near future to reconsider its present position, it would seem likely that the amplified form of certificate will come into general use. Clients whose securities are listed on a stock exchange, and who must therefore file reports annually with the Commission, would probably wish to have the identical form of certificate used in such reports and in their published reports to stockholders. This in turn seems likely to lead to the use of the amplified form of certificate in reports to stockholders, or other interested parties, of companies whose securities are not listed. Such clients would presumably wish to have the auditor's certificate in their case read similarly to that appearing in the published reports of large companies of high standing in the business world. Here, too, as in respect of other matters of interest to the independent auditor, provisions of the securities acts and the regulatory requirements of the Securities and Exchange Commission will tend to influence the standards of accounting practice, not only in the case of companies coming within the Commission's jurisdiction but in the business and financial world generally.

Consistency of Application of Accounting Principles

In my opinion one of the most important statements ever included in an auditor's report or certificate was one which was made part of the form promulgated by the Institute in 1934. The accountant's opinion thereafter was to indicate whether the financial statements fairly presented the company's position and results of operations "in accordance with accepted principles of accounting consistently maintained by the company during the year under review." One of the explanatory notes for the use of the new form of certificate made it clear that the mention of consistency had particular reference to consistency in basis with that for the preceding year, and emphasized that if there has been any material change, either in accounting principles or in the manner of their application, the nature of the change should be indicated.

As one analyzes the nature of so-called accounting principles, it becomes evident that consistency in their application, coupled with disclosure of any change which appears warranted, is in a sense even more important than in the selection or application of a principle or one of its variations in a given case. Accounting "principles," as understood by the practicing accountant, mean as stated in one of Webster's definitions, "a general or settled rule or ground of action." Such principles are born out of reasoning from circumstances to a practical conclusion, and out of the experience of businessmen and accountants.

In considering accounting principles and their application, cognizance may well be taken of the following observations by President Emeritus Lowell of Harvard University in his book on *Conflicts of Principle*, written during the past decade:

> What appears as a universal principle is in fact often true only within the limits of the conditions in which it is properly applied, and becomes partially true, or altogether inapplicable, under new and unfamiliar circumstances. Yet we find a difficulty in emancipating ourselves from a conviction of its absoluteness and tend to rely upon it as an infallible guide where it is so no longer. . . .
>
> Considerations like these induce one to reflect upon the limited nature of principles commonly accepted as universal; upon the conflicts that arise when two inconsistent principles of that kind come into collision; and how far such conflicts may be avoided by recognizing that there are limits, with a debatable region in which neither can be rigorously applied.
>
> . . . Without attempting to assert that there are no propositions of absolutely universal application, it is enough for our purpose to say that many are commonly stated as universal when in fact they are not. . . .[1]

Although what I have quoted from President Lowell was written with quite a different purpose from that for which I have referred to it, I believe it has pertinency because of its caution against regarding a "principle" as being necessarily universal and capable of only one application. An accounting example of wide variation in application is the principle of "cost or market, whichever is lower" for determining the inventory amount to be used in stating both balance sheet and income statement. "Cost" in such case may be arrived at by a variety of methods, among them: specific costs, average cost, first-in — first-out, and last-in — first-out. Any one of these methods may be appropriate in a given situation, and in some situations the circumstances may be such that more than one may be suitably used.

[1] Cambridge, Harvard University Press, 1932, pp. 4, 5, 10.

It is at this point that consistency of application becomes vital. If the same cost method be followed from year to year the operating results, in so far as they are affected by the inventories at beginning and end of each fiscal period, are on a comparable basis. If, however, the inventory at the end of one period (and consequently for the beginning of the next period) has been stated on the basis of first-in — first-out, and at the end of the next period on the basis of last-in — first-out, the results of operations shown in the income statements of the two periods will certainly not be on a comparable basis and may be positively misleading. In such a case there must be disclosure of the change of basis and if the statements are to be truly informing, the income statement relating to the year of change should give, at least approximately, the effect of the change of basis. Also, in the auditor's certificate the change will have to be noted as an exception to the consistency of application of accepted principles of accounting, even though the change in inventory practice may be one of which he heartily approves.

The shift in emphasis from the balance sheet to the income statement, which has been so noticeable during the past two decades, has placed a premium on consistency in applying accounting principles to the stating of financial position and, especially, to the determination of operating results, and on the importance of adequate disclosure when a material departure from consistency has occurred, even though there may have been good reason therefor.

Audit Limitations

Forty years ago only a small percentage of business concerns had their accounts regularly audited. Today practically all companies with any public interest have periodical audits, either because it is required by statute or other applicable regulations, or because it has become recognized as good business practice. Today many companies in which there is little or no direct public interest follow the same practice. Even in the minds of those who are clients of the professional auditor, there has at times been a lack of understanding of just what should be the scope of the audit in normal circumstances and the purposes of having the statements "certified."

To many a layman "an audit is an audit," and many may have tacitly assumed that the work of the accountant involved verification or review of all the recorded transactions of the year. If some irregularity occurred in the petty cash, why didn't the auditor discover it? An irregularity of larger amount which, as a result of collusion or of other untoward circumstances, was not detected in the course of an audit of ordinary scope may have led to the query, why wasn't it discovered by the auditor?

It is well to bear in mind that no matter how ready the accountant may be to bear all the responsibilities that are properly his, there are practical limitations on both the scope and results of an audit conducted in normal circumstances and for the purpose of certifying the financial statements of a business corporation. In the first place, with the growth of business concerns during the last half century, it is obvious that for the great majority of them it is not a practical proposition to examine the records of all the transactions which have occurred during the year. Thus as a practical development has arisen the practice already discussed of making audits on the basis of testing and sampling the accounts, and with considerable reliance on the system of internal check and control.

With the widespread public interest in business enterprises today, the review of the accounting policies followed by a corporation and the determination whether its accounts represent the consistent application of sound accounting principles are recognized as of outstanding importance, and this part of the accountant's work may consume a considerable part of the time devoted to a given engagement. It is significant that in the course of the seven years during which the Securities and Exchange Commission has been reviewing the registration statements filed with it under the Securities Act (security issues) and the Securities Exchange Act (security listings and corporate annual reports) the questions which the Commission has raised regarding financial statements have in only a few instances been the result of financial irregularities as such but have dealt largely with the propriety or otherwise of the application of accounting principles to various circumstances and transactions of the registrants.

The necessity for recognizing both the value and the limitations of an audit was well stated in an address by Mr. George O. May fifteen years ago, when speaking to the Society of Certified Public Accountants of the State of New Jersey on the subject of "A Proper Courage in the Assumption of Responsibility by the Accountant." Mr. May, whose brilliant mind and wise counsel have served the profession so well, said *inter alia:*

> . . . An audit is a safeguard; the maintenance of this safeguard entails an expense; and this expense can be justified only if the value of the safeguard is found to be fully commensurate with its cost. The cost of an audit so extensive as to be a complete safeguard would be enormous and far beyond any value to be derived from it. A superficial audit is dangerous because of the sense of false security which it creates. Between the two extremes there lies a mean at which the audit abundantly justifies its cost.
>
> The problem is to determine this happy mean, to insure that the auditor does not fall short of a reasonable discharge of his duties, and the investor or lender does not attribute to the audit a greater significance than it can, as a practical matter, possess. And it must be recognized that skilled dishonesty, especially collusive dishonesty, may at times and for a time deceive even the auditor who conducts what is regarded as a reasonable audit, and that this should be so is not to be regarded as a defect in the system, since, as I have said, audit procedure represents a balancing of the consideration of risks on the one side and

cost on the other. As a matter of fact, investors and lenders need protection against deliberate dishonesty less than protection against unsound practices and undue optimism. . . .

It will be noted from the foregoing quotation that the final determination of what is a reasonable scope of an examination which will serve as a basis for an expression of the auditor's opinion in financial statements must rest on his judgment.

The practical limitations on an audit were well stated in a report by the Stock List Subcommittee on Independent Audits and Audit Procedure of the New York Stock Exchange in August, 1939. After emphasizing the importance of that part of the accountant's work which relates to the application of sound accounting principles to the factual data which form the base of the financial statements, the Subcommittee went on to discuss the audit phase of the accountant's work, as follows:

. . . In the case of large modern companies, the aggregate expense to industry of extremely detailed examinations of the voluminous material, by independent accountants, would be out of all proportion to the possible benefits to be gained in the occasional detection of irregularities in a few concerns. Most companies are honestly run, and the huge expense which would be incurred by all for detection of occasional misrepresentations in the few would in the aggregate be an economic waste to investors and to the public.

Even when this cost is not weighed in relation to American business as a whole, but only in relation to a single large modern concern, it is doubtful if even a most detailed examination would be a complete safeguard. The recent audit of McKesson & Robbins ordered by the Trustee following disclosure of the Coster-Musica frauds is probably one of the most detailed audits ever made of a large industrial concern by independent public accountants. Independent engineers were retained to examine and test check the quantity, quality and pricing of the inventory and many months were spent in an examination of hundreds of thousands of items and tens of thousands of pages of records. Even this audit could not cover all transactions, and the independent auditor's report included the customary phrase: "But we did not make a detailed audit of the transactions." We mention this only to indicate the burden which would be placed on corporations if all transactions were to be audited in detail.

The May, 1939, issue of the *Journal of Accountancy* contained an editorial in which consideration was given to the paper by Dr. Jules I. Bogen on "An Objective Appraisal of the Independent Audit," to which paper reference was made earlier in these lectures.[1] The editor summed up the matter succinctly when he said:

> Two courses are open to the (accounting) profession, and we believe that both are being followed: (1) continually to extend and improve auditing procedure so far as it may be reasonable and practicable to do so; (2) to educate the public to an understanding of auditing, and the essential, unavoidable limitations of the work of auditors.[2]

The latter course is in some ways the more difficult of the two. The American Institute of Accountants is diligently carrying on this effort for the education of the investing public. Its two pamphlet publications, *Financial Statements — What They Mean* and *Accounting and Your Pocketbook*, are useful contributions toward this end.

Accounting Research

One of the important, as well as significant, developments in the field of accounting in the last few years is the establishment of the Bureau of Research by the American Institute of Accountants. The Committee on Accounting Procedure of the Institute has the responsibility for directing the work of the accounting research bureau and for issuing the bulletins which set forth the opinions or conclusions of the Committee in respect of matters which have been the subject of study. A director of research is in immediate charge of this work. Dr. T. H. Sanders, a member of the faculty of the Harvard Graduate School of Business

[1] See p. 17.
[2] Vol. LXVII, No. 5, p. 259.

Administration, is serving in this capacity and has rendered valuable service in the planning and initiation of the research program.[1]

This research activity of the Institute arose from the conviction on the part of practitioners that it would be helpful to the profession, in considering principles or rules of practice where a diversity of procedure had developed, even when alternative practices were recognized as having justification in different circumstances, to narrow the diversity and, so far as possible, to find a basis for a principle or rule of universal application.

The matters which form the subject of research or consideration by the Institute's Committee on Accounting Procedure have a very direct relation to the work of the auditor because they bear on the basis for the opinion expressed in the standard form of short report that the statements present fairly the position of the concern and the results of operations "in conformity with generally accepted accounting principles." It is for the purpose of seeking clarification of, and as far as possible unity in the application of, principles that research activities are being carried on.

A number of important subjects which have been studied by the Bureau of Accounting Research and the Institute Committee have been covered by bulletins thus far issued by the Committee. As illustrations of the research activities of the Institute, reference may be made to three subjects, two of them where definite conclusions were expressed and another where the subject is still "in work." One of the two matters first referred to is that of foreign operations and foreign exchange on which a bulletin was issued in December, 1939. This bulletin was in response to a need arising out

[1] Since these lectures were delivered Dr. Sanders has resigned in order to enter upon war service at Washington. The present director of research is Professor James L. Dohr, a member of the faculty of the School of Business at Columbia University.

of a situation which had been cumulating for some years prior to the outbreak of the present war but which became still more acute after September, 1939, and which called for prompt consideration so that the Committee's views might come to the members of the Institute and the profession at large in time for use in examinations to be made of 1939 financial statements. It is encouraging to note that, although there has at times been criticism of the deliberation with which accountants reach a conclusion in matters where differences of opinion exist, it was possible in the particular instance to consider the situation with dispatch, to formulate various suggestions for dealing with the problem, and to reach conclusions which could be made the subject of a bulletin to the members of the Institute.

When, in the early part of the twentieth century, consolidated balance sheets and income accounts came rapidly into general use by corporations having subsidiaries, no distinction was observed between domestic and foreign subsidiaries. It was the general assumption, and quite justifiably so in the circumstances of the times, that the same basic consideration which made the inclusion of the accounts of one or more domestic subsidiaries in consolidated statements desirable similarly made the inclusion of foreign subsidiaries desirable. At that time there were no substantial restrictions on trade in any part of the world and between different nations, with the exception of tariffs, the effect of which was generally understood. Currency restrictions were practically unknown at that time, and currencies in general commercial use had a reasonably well-established value which did not fluctuate widely in their relation to each other. Relatively slight exchange fluctuations had the effect of starting the flow of gold in one direction or the other so that a corrective process was promptly set in motion. In these circumstances the business activities, the availability of profits for distribution, and the realizability of assets in the liquidation of a business were not fundamentally different in the case of foreign subsidiaries from subsidiaries operating in the home country.

During the decade immediately following the First World War there were radical fluctuations in currency values, and this introduced an added risk and difficulty in carrying on business in foreign countries. Even at that, however, the consolidating of accounts of foreign subsidiaries with those of the parent company in the published statements was in large part continued, though some questions began to be raised as to whether a distinction between the business of foreign and domestic subsidiaries had not developed which might make a different method of treatment desirable. In the 1930's the blocking of currencies and other restrictions on foreign business and foreign investments caused the question to become more acute. When war broke out in September, 1939, there were still further restrictions and still greater uncertainties as to the status of foreign investments and the availability of profits that might be apparently earned by foreign subsidiaries. The time had clearly arrived to reconsider the propriety of including the results of operations and the assets and liabilities of foreign subsidiaries or branches in the consolidated statements of American companies in the same manner as had been generally followed in the past. It was evident that, had the same conditions existed a generation ago (when consolidated statements were so rapidly coming into use) as today, it is most unlikely that foreign subsidiaries would have been consolidated in the same manner as domestic subsidiaries. The solution was not so simple, however, as merely untying the knot and putting the situation back in a position where a brand new solution could be generally applied.

The conclusion of the Committee was that disclosure of the essential facts was of the essence of any solution. Consequently, the following alternatives were suggested:

(a) To exclude foreign subsidiaries from consolidation and to furnish: (1) statements in which only domestic subsidiaries would be consolidated; and (2) as to foreign subsidiaries, a summary in suitable form of their assets and liabilities, their income and losses for the year, and the parent company's equity therein. The aggregate amount of investments in foreign subsidiaries should be shown separately, and the basis on which the amount was arrived at should be stated. If these investments include any amount of surplus of foreign subsidiaries and such surplus had previously been included in consolidated surplus, the amount should be separately shown or earmarked in stating the consolidated surplus in the statements here suggested. The exclusion of foreign subsidiaries from consolidation does not make it permissible to include inter-company profits which would be eliminated if such subsidiaries were consolidated.

(b) To consolidate domestic and foreign subsidiaries as hitherto, and to furnish in addition the summary described in (a) (2) above.

(c) To furnish: (1) complete consolidated statements, and also (2) consolidated statements for domestic companies only.

(d) To consolidate domestic and foreign subsidiaries as hitherto, and to furnish in addition parent company statements showing investment in and income from foreign subsidiaries separate from those of domestic subsidiaries.[1]

The second of the two matters above referred to is that of depreciation on appreciation of fixed assets. Considerable diversity in depreciation treatment had arisen during the decade of the 1920's when the practice of reflecting on the books apparent appreciation in property value reached its peak. Some concerns charged into the income statement of each period a depreciation allowance based on the appreciated or written-up value, but probably the greater number charged into the income statement only that part of the depreciation allowance which related to the cost of the property, and charged against the revaluation surplus (set up when the write-up for the appreciation was made) that part of the depreciation allowance which related to the appre-

[1] *Accounting Research Bulletins*, No. 4 (December, 1939), "Foreign Operations and Foreign Exchange," pp. 30–31.

ciation. Sometimes the full amount of the depreciation allowance on the written-up value was charged to current operations, but before stating the net income for the period a credit was brought into the income statement by transfer thereto of a portion of the revaluation surplus equivalent to the portion of the depreciation allowance for the current fiscal period relating to the appreciation reflected in the accounts.

In its bulletin on this subject the Committee took the definite position that ordinarily it is not desirable that property values be written up in the accounts but that, if for special reasons this nevertheless be done, it then follows that depreciation allowances on the full appreciated property amounts should be charged to operations. This pronouncement of the Committee appears to have been generally accepted in the profession.

Another subject which is being studied by the research bureau is the accounting treatment of inventories from both the balance sheet and the income statement points of view. Preliminary statements on the subject by the research bureau have appeared in the *Journal of Accountancy* for June and October, 1940, and the results of a questionnaire circulated among the members of the Institute's committee on accounting procedure were published in the April, 1941, issue of the *Journal*. The results of the questionnaire indicated that considerable further study would be necessary for the purpose of clarifying the numerous considerations entering into the accounting treatment of inventories and of stating more definitely the basic inventory principles and the procedures for their application in the accounting treatment of inventories.

IV. CONCLUSION

In bringing to a close this dissertation on auditing development during the first forty years of the twentieth century, and in considering the duty of the independent auditor in the years ahead, I cannot do better than to refer once more to the writings of Sir Arthur Lowes Dickinson. He closed his book on *Accounting Practice and Procedure* with the following paragraphs:

> In concluding this review of accounting practice and procedure, and the duties and responsibilities of the public accountant in relation thereto, it may not be out of place to call attention to the mental qualifications required by one who essays to attack and determine accounting problems.
>
> These are: ability, coupled with tact and honesty, to ascertain facts without friction and with impartiality; a mind unbiased by previous conceptions, and free to reach independent and reliable conclusions of fact; and a will strong enough to maintain such conclusions against the arguments, opinions, or desires of opponents interested in some opposite or inconsistent conclusion, and yet to adapt such parts of their arguments as may throw new light on the questions at issue. With such qualities, and with the added technical training and practical experience which are equally necessary, the individual is in fact an accountant qualified to deal with the many questions herein discussed, and to add new principles to those which it has been the endeavor to illustrate and explain in this volume.[1]

What I have just quoted from Sir Arthur is as vital and timely today as when it was first written over a quarter century ago.

[1] New York, The Ronald Press Company, 1920 (Sixth Printing), p. 249.

Bei Fragen zur Produktsicherheit wenden Sie sich bitte an:
If you have any questions regarding product safety,
please contact:

Walter de Gruyter GmbH
Genthiner Straße 13
10785 Berlin
productsafety@degruyterbrill.com